THE VOLCANOES ABOVE US

Norman Lewis was born in the North London suburb of Enfield. He was written twelve novels and seven non-fiction works. *A Dragon Apparent* and *Golden Earth* are considered classics of travel, and *Naples '44* has been described as one of the ten outstanding books about the Second World War. His most recent work, *The Missionaries*, was published in 1988 to universal acclaim.

The March of The Long Shadows

Norman Lewis

THE VOLCANOES ABOVE US

ARENA

An Arena Book
Published by Arrow Books Limited
62-65 Chandos Place, London WC2N 4NW

An imprint of Century Hutchinson Ltd

London Melbourne Sydney Auckland
Johannesburg and agencies throughout
the world

First published by Jonathan Cape Ltd 1957
Penguin Books edition 1959
Panther Books edition 1969
Arena edition 1989

Made and printed in Great Britain by
The Guernsey Press Co. Ltd.,
Guernsey, Channel Islands.

ISBN 0 09 960530 9

AUTHOR'S NOTE

While the astute reader may discover certain accidental similarities between fictitious revolution described in this book and the actual events which took place in Guatemala in 1954, this is because all Central American revolutions — of which there have been more than fifty since the turn of the century — are basically similar. The characters do not possess, so far as I know, even accidental resemblance to any living persons, since they are entirely from the imagination.

'Do you say that the waters of the volcano will entrap you again? I command you not to despair. Are not all our people here in New Spain threatened by the volcanoes above us?'

(Extract from a letter from the Archbishop of Mexico written in 1541 to the alcaldía of the ancient Guatemalan capital of Almalonga, after the town had been destroyed by an eruption of water from the volcano *Agua*, – *Bibliografía Mexicana del Siglo XVI.*)

THE VOLCANOES ABOVE US

I

Two weeks after the Mexicans had taken me to the gaol in Merida a warder came in one morning and threw me a copy of the *Heraldo de Yucatán* with a front-page splash about the revolution.

There was going to be a revolution in Guatemala across the border. The paper did not state this as a possibility but as a definite and pre-arranged fact, as if speaking of an exceptional bullfight or a football match — say Guadalajara versus Mexico City. In perhaps a week's time, said the paper, a military uprising would be staged, and this would receive prompt support from columns of Guatemalan refugees and international volunteers who would invade the country at several points from across the southern frontier. The paper was sarcastic about the purity of the revolutionaries' motives and their chances of success. But this was to be expected because it had a left-wing backing, and sympathized with Werner, the dictator of Guatemala. According to his own propaganda Werner was a progressive liberal, and according to almost everyone else he was the bloodiest of bloody-minded Reds.

So now Werner's turn had come. Off-hand, I could not think of a single Latin-American dictator whose fate it had been to die quietly in bed in the land in which he had been born. They came to power to make, or to keep, their country safe for foreign investments, and in the course of doing this they usually managed to turn it into something like a private farm. They lived blandly aloof behind the slogans and the parades and the shoulder-holstered guns of the men who walked always at their sides, until eventually — apart from a few who escaped to seedy oblivion across the border — they fell riddled with bullets fired from some unsuspected quarter. After which, the mask snatched away, the world was told of the horded loot, the harems of young girls, the fabulous rackets, and the torture chambers. And by this time, of course, the new man was already in position, smiling sweetly, his pockets full of promised reforms.

Werner's case was somewhat different. His coming to power five years back had followed the traditional slaughter, but there had been a failure to look after foreign investments. At first he had shown unusual promise. But then he was supposed to have taken to the study of Marx and Lenin in the hope of picking up tips on the art of attaching the support of the masses to a shaky regime. And in the end he had come to believe more than was healthy for him of what he read. Werner had also driven the country too hard and too fast and — in the way they do in Guatemala — he had killed his enemies when he could. Now the enemies who had managed to get away were closing in on him, and I supposed that sooner or later, also in Guatemalan style, they would kill him.

As one of Werner's minor victims I was not particularly unhappy to read this news, although I couldn't see any way it was likely to affect me for better or for worse. In accordance with the rationing system I imposed on myself I read only the bare details. After that I went through the Situations Vacant, Social Life and 'Necrologia', and then I allowed myself two exciting items on the second page: one about a woman who had shot a ten-year-old boy for stealing her mangoes in Ciudad Carmen, thereby starting an important riot, and another of a plane that had crashed in the Sierras when one of the dangerous lunatics it was carrying had attacked the pilot. Before I had time to turn my attention to the details of what was predicted for Guatemala, a visitor called to see me.

I remember the man principally by his wonderfully laundered shirt, worn loose over his trousers in the Mexican manner. He put a soft, brown, scrupulous hand on my shoulder and told me that he was shocked to find an educated man in my position. After that, he made a few complimentary remarks, smiling past me at an invisible third person with whom he was on a confident and affectionate standing. He knew something of my background it seemed. 'You English planters were the best in our country.' Our friend was a Guatemalan, by the way, but he spoke good English by local standards.

I thanked him. 'Extremely kind of you to say so,' I said. We talked about the vices and the virtues of the various foreigners that get a living out of Guatemala. I told him that I thought the Germans were very good too, in their own way — painstaking and thorough in their methods as you would expect them to be. 'I think you were better than the Germans. That is my opinion. I think that my country cannot afford to lose you. How did you leave your coffee finca?'

'I didn't leave it. It left me. It was reformed under Werner's agrarian new deal. I was offered about a twentieth of what it was worth, and when I didn't accept they reformed it all the same.'

The Guatemalan clicked his tongue sympathetically. 'The one who has gained from this is certainly Werner. He has taken your finca and he put all the money in his pocket. It is a very bad thing for us that you must go. All you English were good. You were interested to improve the land. Our own people — well, to tell you the truth they will wear out the land and then let it go. This man has done very bad things for us.'

My friend certainly hated Werner, and he had the typical Guatemalan upper-class admiration for all foreigners and a deep and sincere belief in the spinelessness and lack of character of his own people. After he had called Werner a few hard names I guessed what he was — an agent of the revolutionaries on the look-out for likely recruits, and making a start by combing the prisons. The Mexicans hadn't told him that I was being held for what was more or less a technical infringement, and I thought he looked disappointed when he found out that it was not for armed robbery or some other serious crime. The revolutionaries had a lot to offer for nothing. Or almost for nothing. Things with not a great deal of value, like a commission in the revolutionary army, and very valuable things indeed, including freedom and a guarantee that my finca would be returned. The finca? — oh, that certainly. Why, of course . . . And naturally, there would be no fighting. Like all wars and revolts this was to be a walk-over. 'How can he fight when he has nothing, no aviones, no tanks, no cannons? We go in. In three days it is all over. It is nothing, nothing, trivial, insignificant.'

Like the present little matter of smuggling antiques out of Mexico had been, I remembered — a very trivial thing indeed when the idea had first been presented to me.

But what was the alternative? I was in a Mexican gaol — a predicament indeed. The Mexicans are absorbed in the problem of the criminal's reform. The first day they put you in prison they weigh you, and after that they weigh you again every week. If you begin to lose weight a psychiatrist comes and explains to you how to adjust your personality to the facts of captivity, and if you don't start to put on flesh again he shows by his manner that he is hurt. The cells in the best Mexican prisons are fitted up to make you feel as if you were in a sanatorium. There are cheerful mottoes, and there is not an iron bar to be seen, while the civilized arrangement by which married prisoners are allowed regular co-habitation with their wives has been admired by all students of modern penology. This enlightened system has naturally produced a few problems for the authorities, the chief one being how to prevent people committing unimportant crimes so as to get themselves lodged and fed at the State's expense in a style they could never aspire to as law-abiding citizens. The great disadvantage of the system is that it is rather harder to get out of a Mexican prison — even if you are only being held on suspicion — than out of those in other less idealistic countries. You may wait a year while your dossier is being prepared for the case to go for trial — or just as long before they decide to release you through lack of evidence. Although all the Mexican prison officials are kind and sympathetic in their attitude, the uncertainty and the long delays are hard on the nerves.

The Guatemalan played on my fears expertly. He prowled round the cell with a pantherish flexing of the knees, and turned the wash-tap on and off, whistling with admiration. His shirt gleamed like the whites of a young negress's eyes. 'The trouble is they might forget about you,' he suggested. 'You don't want to stay here for ever, do you?' A dose of prison turns a man into a pessimist. I was quite ready to believe him. 'You must ask to be allowed to change your plea to guilty,' he said. 'We shall pay your fine, and you will be deported. In three days' time.' I could see he didn't think much of me as a potential desperado, but I had at least fought in one war and knew Guatemala as well as most Guatemalans. He offered me a hundred dollars a week with a bonus of five hundred on demobilization, which I later found out was what they paid Cubans, and half what Europeans and North Americans were supposed to get. I found myself holding a paper which my friend was urging me to sign. But I couldn't make up my mind on the spur of the moment. I asked him to give me time to think, and he was very understanding and told me that he would come and see me again next day. When I heard the neat, decisive sound of the cell door close behind him I was sorry. I was soon tormenting myself with the thought that he might not come back after all, and this put me into such a panic that I couldn't touch the evening beans brought by my amiable warder.

Next morning when the Guatemalan came again I signed the paper. I had passed a bad night and I would have signed away anything in exchange for the promise of freedom. He snatched the paper from me and put it in his pocket. A perfunctory hand-grasp and he was gone. This was enough to produce another crop of misgivings, although I had committed myself now, and it was too late to do anything about it.

I spent the rest of that day trying to get the recent years into perspective, and I wondered if I wasn't going downhill rather fast. Five years ago I had owned two thousand hectares of the best coffee-growing land in the Guatemalan highlands — a property which had been in my family for over seventy years, and which the government had virtually expropriated, leaving me faced with certain clear-cut alternatives. If I were to cling to any hope of ever recovering my estate I must stay on — be on the spot. I must fight, persuade, bribe, struggle to gain the ear of important people, wait patiently for a change of government. To do this I needed money, and I had to live. This was the great problem. In Central America there are land-owners and the wretched peones that work for them. There are professions which are barred to foreigners — such as politics — and several others in which they cannot hope to succeed, like shopkeeping. It is a question of finding enough capital to open a cinema, a soda-fountain, or a hotel — there is always room for one more of these. If there isn't this kind of money available, the thing to do — it is what practically every foreigner does — is to invest in some crack-brain undertaking and fail picturesquely. I bought a boatload of lobsters to sell in Miami for six hundred per cent profit — but the refrigeration failed and the lobsters were bad when we got there. After that I dabbled with what I had left in the British Honduras currency racket, and from this grey-market enterprise I passed by easy and natural stages into the black market and worse. Six months ago I had come to be engaged in smuggling out of Mexico antiques that had almost certainly been looted from the ancient tombs. Now I was in prison, and in order to get out I was going to join up with a gang of international adventurers.

How much of this was sheer bad luck — and how much had I brought on myself? That was the question.

———————

2

THREE days later I was released from prison, taken by the police to the airport and put on the Pan-American plane bound for Tegucigalpa, capital of the Republic of Honduras. Here I became a lieutenant in General Balboa's Army of Liberation, which was forming in camps round the city.

Tegucigalpa at this time was full of shark-fishers, pearlers, students of the occult, men who were going to sail round the world on balsa rafts, men who had seen flying saucers, claimants to Polish titles, explorers who had located the lost gold mines of the Cuna Indians of Panama, divers who had charted the position of bullion-laden wrecks in shallow water. The papers had been instructed always to refer to us as 'heroic crusaders in the Guatemalan people's struggle for liberty', and we had one thing in common, an infinite capacity for self-delusion. The Hondurans treated us with great kindness and courtesy. The men hugged and kissed us in the streets, although they kept their womenfolk out of sight when we visited them in their homes. At night they surrounded our camp with police armed with machine-guns. These precautions did not prevent one-third of our number falling victims to venereal disease before we were given twenty-five dollars apiece, American war-surplus uniforms all made to fit the same fat man with a dwarf's legs, a purple banner per company embroidered with hearts and daggers, and so they sent us down to the frontier. Here in the tropics at the height of the rainy season, it rained for several hours daily, and a third of those that V.D. had spared were shortly sent back to the capital suffering from malaria. Discontent developed among the troops when it was discovered that the bulk of the rations consisted of macaroni letters of the alphabet. Villagers sold us cactus-alcohol which caused several cases of temporary blindness. A dangerous rift opened between the Patriots — Guatemalan refugees — who refused to fight except under their own commanders and who had declared they would accept no reward for their services, and the rest of us who were, after all, only mercenaries. This antipathy was only prevented from developing into a small side-war by the news that the invasion was on.

We received this information from a bird-voiced lady announcer of Radio Tegucigalpa, who told us that, well supported by planes and tanks, we had crossed the frontier and penetrated deeply into Guatemalan territory and were hourly expected to occupy the important town of Chiquimula, where an uprising in our favour had taken place.

The facts, as we later learned them from *Time* magazine, were as follows. Werner had postponed mobilization and was still awaiting a reply to his appeal to the United Nations when, on the morning of that day, the four pilots we used to see hanging about the bars in Tegucigalpa had gone into action. These four men used to make a great thing about not saying where they came from, but they looked, talked and acted like Americans. That morning they took off in their Thunderbolts and ripped the bellies out of the tanks at Puerto de San José where President Werner kept his oil supplies. They next flew up to Guatemala City and dropped five hundred-pound bombs on forts built in 1850 to hold off the attacks of Indian irregular cavalry. (The Army of Liberation's radio station told the people in Guatemala City when they would be coming, and they were there on the dot with all the population waiting for them on the rooftops.)

After that they derailed a few trains, flattened a few strategic villages, shot up a few peasants in uniform, and then — as it didn't seem as if there was going to be much in the way of opposition — they went back to Tegucigalpa and settled down in the bars again.

You might say that these four pilots won the war between them, although camped in our steaming jungle we were quite unaware that they had done so. It was the nineteenth century against the twentieth — pre-atomic. We might as well have stayed where we were or have gone back without any further waste of time to our lost treasures and our balsa rafts. But we were an Army of Liberation, and we had to liberate something, so — urged on by the young lady broadcaster of Radio Tegucigalpa — we plunged into the unmapped five thousand square miles of jungle along Guatemala's southern frontier and began our painful and unnecessary invasion.

The column to which I belonged numbered six hundred men and was commanded by a Colonel Kranz, an ageing German officer — ex-S.S. — who lived by encouraging Latin-American militarists in the belief that he was a Nazi war-criminal; very ruthless and efficient. Our column was officered by the Patriots and Mercenaries already described. The other ranks were Indians who had to be encouraged, with some difficulty, to develop a useful hostility towards a man — Werner — who had distributed among them a lot of land. Casualties, at first, were few. Within half an hour of the advance's getting under way, our only tank went down like a submerging hippopotamus in a swamp, and two Indians were drowned. Two more Indians fell through a liana bridge they were testing — they were swept into some rapids, and could not be rescued. Another Indian died from snake-bite, and another went mad after eating too much of an intoxicating fungus. Among the non-Indians there were no casualties until the last stages of our march, and then only when we had the incredibly bad luck to run into a retreating enemy patrol. The chances against this happening when both sides were doing their best to avoid each other in practically limitless jungle were almost incalculably slight. But it happened.

It happened on the seventh day of our advance. Our column had formed originally into three groups: an advance party, the main body and the rearguard. Kranz would have liked to do the thing in orthodox fashion, with reconnaissance patrols, and parties covering the flanks, but the jungle decided against this. We burrowed stolidly ahead through the tangled undergrowth and the rain, like some insect gnawing its way blindly through rotten wood, and as the days went by we lost shape and cohesion as a force. Indians went in front hacking a path through the forest with their machetes, and in the rear came more Indians carrying the camp equipment; the crates full of alphabetical macaroni, the ammunition, and finally — when nearly a week had gone by and we had seen nothing that lived but birds — most of the guns. Any of us who had lived in Central America believed that Indians were more comfortable and happy when they were well loaded, and we were familiar with the story that an Indian returning from market preferred loading his pack with stones to travelling with nothing on his back. The Indians who cleared the way ahead of us used their machetes with the precision of machines, working at the pace they were accustomed to, never faster or slower, but usually rather too fast for the rest of the column that straggled on after them, sometimes falling miles behind.

On the morning of the seventh day we learned from the young lady announcer of Radio Tegucigalpa that the revolution was over, and she congratulated us on our splendid victory. Werner had gone, handing over the government to one of the army chiefs who had asked for an armistice. When this news came through the last of the rifles were

19

strapped on to the backs of the Indian porters bringing up the rear. I was with the advance party and at midday we were held up by a river with too much water in it for us to wade across. We had to go upstream about a mile before we found a place narrow enough for the Indians to throw a liana bridge across. When this had been done about thirty Indians and five Patriots went across, leaving ten of us on the near-side to keep contact with the main body.

As soon as they reached the further bank they were surrounded by the enemy force who must have been stalking us as we came up the river. It was an informal, almost conversational occurrence. We, who were left behind, cut away our end of the bridge and dropped down out of sight among some rocks. We managed to do this unseen, although a child could have thrown a stone from where we were hiding into the little assembly of men on the other bank. We could hear the Patriots arguing with the officer commanding the enemy patrol, who was dressed in white cottons like an Indian, but wore epaulets. It was as if the Patriots had something to sell to this officer which he was not in the slightest interested in buying. He listened in a detached and bored way to the quietly persistent sales arguments, but remained unconvinced. He really didn't want this particular piece of merchandise and there was no amount of further recommendation on the part of the Patriots that would induce him to change his mind. He shrugged his shoulders and, turning his head away from the anxious salesman's clamour, he gave an order. I could not hear what he said, but the Patriots began to unbuckle their belts with their pistols and lay them in a pile. Afterwards they started to argue again. They all spoke at once, very rapidly and excitedly, and they gesticulated a great deal. When they stopped and seemed to be waiting for a reply the enemy officer spoke a few words, quietly and without heat. He had a small, dark face and much more Indian than white blood. The only words that reached me of what he had to say were *no lo creo* — 'I don't believe it'. This, it seems, was in answer to the Patriots' protestations that the fighting was over. Our Indians, as usual, had nothing to say.

After that the Regular Army officer made the prisoners form a small circle, all facing inwards. He seemed hard to please. He gestured and gave orders in his quiet voice, moving the men about and shuffling their positions until it suited him. After three or four attempts he seemed satisfied. Our men now formed a small, tight circle facing inwards, and the enemy officer had placed one of his own men behind each one of ours, and thrown round them a second, more widely spaced ring of his men. The Patriots were still arguing and trying to explain the military situation, and our Indians were as silent as ever, their heads hanging. The Regular officer lit a cigarette, drew at it a few times and threw it away. He gave an order and the ring of men immediately behind ours drew their machetes and slashed at the tendons behind our men's knees. As they struck, the Patriots cried out in agonized surprise. Some of their utterances seemed very absurd, such as *no quiero esto*, which means, 'I don't want this to happen'. Of course they didn't want it to happen. The Indians appeared to be accepting their fate with their usual submissiveness, and the men with the machetes continued to slash at them, both Patriot and Indian with quick, short strokes, so that sometimes they struck three or four times at a man's legs, almost before he had time to fall. It was as if they were trimming bunches of bananas, and you could hear the dry chop of the machetes all the time. The Indians in the outer ring, waiting with drawn machetes exchanged glances and smiled shyly at each other.

At that moment I vomited. It was not the sickness I had experienced on any other occasion. There was no warning at all and no discomfort. I simply, and as a natural un- premeditated act, emptied the contents of my stomach. I retched twice and looked up again. Most of our men were down now, and through the movements of the executioners I saw them lying, some of them in strangely restful postures. One man, for example, lay almost comfortably on his side, head slightly raised, eyes open and staring in my direction. I wanted to jump up and do something. It was still not too late. Our comrades were broken and crippled, but they could still be healed if only the men with the machetes could be persuaded to stop their work.

But they went on. They were using their machetes without apparent passion or great violence. They were hacking our men in the leisurely, practised way in which they were accustomed to clear a path through the lianas and the thick, juicy stemmed plants of the jungle. Sometimes an Indian would pause to examine his handicraft and then go on to add a few conscientious strokes. It had become a fairly silent operation apart from the sound of the chopping. There was an occasional gurgle but the screams had stopped. I found that my nose was running and my eyes watering as if I were suffering from a violent cold.

Only one man came through the ring of the men working with machetes and shuffled towards the river on elbows and knees. He looked like a clown acting in a poor sort of circus. A soldier noticed him and went after him without hurrying and headed him off. The man on his knees who was facing me only twenty yards away stopped and raised his head to look up, mouth open, at the soldier who was looking down. This man was a Patriot, and I had developed in the past few days a benevolence towards him. I had accepted him as not a bad sort of chap. And now suddenly his personality stood out in high relief. I remembered all about him. I knew him better than my own brother. I remembered the way he liked to tell us about his aristocratic descent, and about the sister whose dowry he was working for. He was a pleasant, mild sort of a chap — a bit of a hypochondriac — who fussed about his health, and was quietly proud of the fact that he developed a patch of eczema every time an insect bit him. I found myself completely unable to accept the fact that this sensitive, vulnerable man who could be put into a panic by an anopheles mosquito, was to die immediately, by a heavy-bladed knife. I would have renounced my hope of getting back my finca to prevent what was going to happen from happening, but the soldier chopped at him softly and economically, and he lay down on his side without a sound, as if he were settling himself for a nap. The whole course of this slow-motion extermination took only a few minutes, but more than an average lifetime's experience of tragedy was forced into it. I thought that probably only a few hundred, or at the most a few thousand, people alive would have felt the sensations that I had just felt, and wondered if it was, as they said, a fallacy that hair could turn white overnight.

That was the first and last of the fighting. The men of the enemy patrol, wiped their machetes on plantain leaves and then they formed up and went off. An hour later our main column came up and we crossed the river, cleaned up the bodies and buried them in a trench. The Patriots were emotional about this task but the Indians who dug the trench and filled it in were quite matter of fact. When they had finished, the Indians made a wooden cross and put it at one end of the trench. They then asked for their day's ration of liquor, drank half of it and poured the rest on the earth. Then we moved off.

Next evening we marched into Zacapa which is on the railway line between Honduras and Guatemala City, and we waited there until they got the trains running. We went up to the capital in comfort.

3

THE column led by Lieutenant-Colonel Kranz was the last to reach Guatemala City. The Victory March and the official ceremony of welcome arranged by the civic authorities for the Army of Liberation had taken place on the day before our arrival, the bars were already running short of liquor and the pretty women were disappearing from the streets. With the support of the Regular Army, General Balboa had already become President. He had formed a government which had been recognized at once by the United States, and the opinion began to spread that while we had done our best, for which the nation was duly grateful, the real agents of liberation had been the regulars who had deserted Werner, thereby leaving him defenceless when the four Thunderbolts began to pay their visits to the capital.

The climate of enthusiasm cooled steadily. When we arrived we were still Heroic Defenders of Liberty. A week later the newspapers were calling us 'the friends who recently showed their willingness to come to our assistance'. After another week we had become 'certain elements at present enjoying the hospitality of this city whose military discipline does not, unhappily, correspond with their undoubted valour'. This allusion was contained in a leading article which recommended that we should be thanked and sent back to wherever we had come from as soon as possible.

We ourselves would have been only too pleased to be paid off and demobilized, but the rumour was that President Balboa had no confidence in the loyalty of the Regular Army, and dared not let us go.

Time magazine reported that the explosion, when it occurred, was touched off as the result of a serious inflation in brothel prices, and that it started as an affray between Regular cadets and Liberation Army men in an establishment called La Locha. I cannot say whether this is so or not, but on the particular afternoon I had been invited to lunch at the house of an old friend of the family who lived on the opposite side of the town from where we were quartered in the Roosevelt Barracks. By this time it was hardly safe for a Liberation Army man to show his face in a bar, or go out after dark.

Don Arturo O'Connell lived in the nearest you could get to a Victorian mansion in an earthquake city of single-storey houses. He was tall, pale and dry; wore tweeds all the year round — which was not impossible when you had been born in the climate — and took a small glass of port after his meals.

Lunch was served as soon as I arrived. It was long-drawn-out and exotic by local standards, and my host was particularly proud of the fact that one of the two vegetables accompanying the meat course was parsnips, which are rare and costly in Central America.

We were both anxious to talk about old times. Don Arturo was one of the oldest members of the foreign colony and had been on intimate terms with both my father and my grandfather. Outside his schooldays in England he had lived the whole of his life in Guatemala and in the normal way he spoke a rapid and slangy local version of Spanish. Unfortunately when in English company he was resolutely British. He refused to speak anything but the language he had first learned at his preparatory school, and as a result his speech was agonizingly slow and punctuated by pauses while he translated his thoughts and groped after the colloquialisms of his youth.

After a number of polite inquiries after persons who didn't particularly interest me, I came to what I was obliged to admit to myself was the real point of my visit.

'By any chance do you hear anything of Greta Herzen these days?' I put this question in my most casual manner.

'Do you mean old Herzen's daughter? The one he had by the squaw?'

'That's right.'

There was a long pause. I tried to maintain a front of unconcern under the probing of Don Arturo's misty eye.

'She went to the bad.' Don Arturo spoke with a kind of sepulchral emphasis. The separation between each deliberately spoken word made it sound like a judgment.

'How was that?' I asked, my throat suddenly dry. I waited again while the old man mustered his lively Spanish thoughts and disciplined them into an order of precise English. Although the news was no more than I could have expected, my day had gone flat.

'Well, as you know. Herzen — ah — pegged out soon after he got back from Europe. What was it now? — T.B. or something of the kind. After that the girl simply ran wild. Rather — ah — a good-looker, I always thought.' He stopped and peered at me suspiciously, 'Weren't you — ah — sweet on her yourself at one time?'

'I don't know. Perhaps I was in a way. I suppose I used to see quite a bit of her when I was in the City off and on.' By the time the old man had got to hear of it the thing must have been common knowledge, I thought.

Don Arturo passed slow judgment again. 'Got mixed up with some — ah — thoroughly bad hats in the end, I'm afraid. Absolute skunks. Just as well for Herzen he didn't live to see the way she turned out. Mind you, it isn't as if all the — ah — Jerries weren't a pretty immoral lot. Personally I could never understand what they could see in the squaws. Well they say it takes all kinds to make a world. Do help yourself to the port.'

I was trying to control the melancholy impatience that had seized me and the sudden claustrophobia induced by the Victorian room, with its slight odour of dust and cats. A young and fierce version of Don Arturo with cocked hat, sword, and tremendous moustaches, dating evidently from the time when he had been His Britannic Majesty's representative in the country, chided me with faded sepia eyes from the wall.

'And now I expect you'll be straining at the leash?'

I made an effort to pull myself together. Don Arturo plodded on. ' — I say you'll be wanting to get down to some real work. Restore the family fortunes — what?'

'That's what I'm here for.' I managed a show of modest confidence.

'How long is it now you've been fighting for your rights? Five years or more, isn't it? And heaven only knows you've had your — ah — whack of bad luck.'

'It was Dad's death,' I said. 'And then the war following immediately afterwards. The point is I was too young to take over, and then when I did . . .'

'The Williamses were stickers, I'll grant them that.' Don Arturo shook his head at a grateful recollection. 'Your grandfather — a splendid chap — ah — any amount of spunk. Don't mean your father wasn't a sound fellow in his way, either. But as for old John Williams — why, the very idea of anyone trying to take his finca away from him is laughable.'

'From what I remember of the old boy I'm certain you're right.'

'Absolutely laughable, I assure you. Why, if it had happened in his time I should have suspected him of being behind this revolution we've just had. He was that kind of man. I mean in your case — well — ah — you could hardly be expected . . .'

'It was all over,' I pointed out, 'almost before I knew what was happening.'

'Of course it was, dear boy. Still, now it's your turn to show us what you can do. Only a question of — ah — buckling to. Eight or ten years' work, naturally enough, before you'll be out of the wood. Ten years at the most, I'd say. Absolutely nothing at all at your age. Youngster like you. Show them the stuff you're made of — what? Ten years, and you'll be on your feet.'

And that I agreed, pretty well summed up the situation. My chance was coming now. I should get the finca back — there was little doubt about that. But when I had got it I must be ready without regrets to sink a period of years into its rehabilitation. And this I was going to do. I would show Don Arturo and the rest of them that our family hadn't to all intents and purposes come to an end with the death of my grandfather.

It was about three in the afternoon when I left the old man and set out on my way back. To be on the safe side I had taken off my Liberation Army armband, but the sloppy uniform gave me away. I was taking it easy and enjoying myself. The outer suburbs of Guatemala City always appealed to me. They are like the last-century frontier towns you see on the screen, but they are painted in all colours; houses and shops and taverns painted blood-red and blue and yellow and strung out in all directions. After a while I began to notice that there was something unusual about this particular afternoon. The doors and the window shutters were closed and there were no half-breeds full of aguardiente sitting in the dirt outside the cantinas. Later I passed three abandoned ice-cream barrows in a row, and

28

while I was wondering about this some Regular Army soldiers came out into the sunshine ahead, and one of them fired a tommy-gun at me. I was surprised, but not very surprised, because there is something in the atmosphere of Guatemala that keeps you in a state of preparation for this kind of thing. People shoot at each other with very little provocation, and frequently — as in this case — they are well out of range.

The outskirts of Guatemala City are seamed with narrow ravines called barrancas, and as this street ran along the edge of one I crossed it and looked over the edge. There was a great deal of garbage in the ravine, both clinging to its sides and in the bottom, with a few black turkey-vultures limping about picking it over. The soldiers were a little nearer now, waddling towards me like circus midgets. The one with the tommy-gun fired another burst and I heard the bullets clink and chirp off the wall ten or fifteen yards ahead.

I swung myself over the low wall and climbed down the slope among the boulders, the tough bushes and the battered oil cans. It occurred to me that shooting had been going on all round, probably for quite a while. But I had been lulled by this relaxing Guatemalan atmosphere into accepting it as part of the rattle and thump of distant ash-can orchestras. I clambered along the uneven bed of the ravine, still going more or less in the same direction.

Here the ravine was thirty or forty feet deep, and I was concealed by the stunted bushes and trees from the street above. It seemed now as though the fighting must be spreading to all parts of the town. I thought I could recognize the stutter of the oerlikon on the Aurora Airfield, and the crump of grenades and mortars coming from the direction of the Roosevelt Hospital. I was not worried enough to overlook the fact that the bottom of the ravine was very disgusting. The rain had left pools of black, stinking water and tame vultures were hobbling about the refuse heaps like rheumaticky hens. There were two dead horses, too, that had

29

died on the street and had been pushed into the ravine, and the small black vultures, which here they call by their old Aztec name of zopilotes, were busy hollowing them out from the rear.

The ravine varied in depth, and there were some places where the bottom was only ten or fifteen feet below the level of the street. Here the sounds of the fighting became clear; the roar of cars being raced through the streets in low gear, the deep cough of the heavy calibre pistols always carried in these countries, and the distant excited shouting that sounded like a lot of ham-actors in a melodrama heard from the gallery of a very big theatre. Then, as the ravine deepened again, the house-roofs fell back behind the skyline, leaving only the tip of a volcano's cone, an occasional quick-fading tatter of tracer smoke, a few startled pigeons in the sky, and then the noises of battle would go out of focus.

It wasn't a simple matter to find one's way through the barrancas. The main system often divided and I sometimes took the wrong fork and went up a side fissure that led nowhere. It took me about two hours to work my way round the town to a point where I estimated that I must be pretty near the Roosevelt Barracks. Here the noise of the fighting was tremendous. I crouched at the top of the bank listening to the explosions and the small-arms fire. It sounded like a regular battle being fought with several thousand on each side, and when I made a cautious appearance above ground level a rifle banged at me from behind a pile of junk a hundred yards away.

After that I gave up. I clambered down the slope again and went back the way I had come until the sound of the shooting quietened in the distance. Then I climbed out of the barranca for the second time and found myself in a pumpkin patch somewhere between Second and Third Streets West. It was peaceful here, and there was no one in sight, so I crossed over to Third Street, and walked up it past the advertising hoardings and the bicycle repair shops, which are a feature of this district, to the Avenida Elena. All this was familiar territory. The next avenue across, running parallel to the Avenida Elena was First Avenue, and I remembered that in the old days I knew a Swiss who ran a pension near the Third Street intersection. It didn't seem specially dangerous to be out in the open in this part of the city. There were no military objectives; nothing important to fight over — only chicken-runs and pumpkin patches and bicycle shops. I could see a few feathers of smoke in the sky over in the direction of the Roosevelt Barracks.

I was very happy to discover that the old Swiss still ran his pension at the same address, and that he remembered me with kindly feeling. The first thing I did was to borrow a civilian suit from him, to be on the safe side, and then I got on the phone to the barracks. Before I left I had received instructions to report to Kranz that evening and I wanted to know what to do. To my surprise they answered immediately and I found myself talking to a Patriot we called Gatito.

'Holà, Gatito,' I said. 'How are things?'

'We are selling our lives dearly. The Liberation Army will never surrender.'

'Do you know what units are involved? Do they have any tanks?' I wanted facts, but Gatito was fighting the battle of the Alamo over again, and he went on with his death song.

' — to the last round of ammunition — the last drop of our blood.'

'It's bad then?'

'The square is littered with the bodies of the fallen. We are awaiting the assault. If necessary we shall die at our posts. Long live the glorious Army of Liberation!'

'Long live the Army of Liberation!' I said. 'Is Kranz there?'

Kranz was undisturbed. I knew he would enjoy this kind

of thing. 'They are burning up energy,' he said. 'It is useful because it reveals mistakes in training. Where are you?'

'In the Swiss place on First Avenue,' I told him.

'I know it. It is honest, but you feed badly. Perhaps you had better stay where you are until I contact you.' There was a faint, distant rattle in the earpiece, like a pneumatic drill breaking up a road-surface a mile away. This was followed by a rumble. 'They're firing at us with unfused shells,' Kranz explained.

'Any signs of the Air Force?'

'I don't worry about it. They couldn't hit anything smaller than the zoological gardens. Well, I must go. Give my love to old Heppler's daughter, and try ringing up again in an hour.'

An hour later the line had gone dead. The shooting stopped at about midnight, and I went to bed. Next morning I was awakened by the sound of men marching past my window, which was at ground level. It was a squad of Liberation Army men being marched away, hands joined on their heads, guarded by regulars with tommy-guns. The regulars were skipping about, snapping at them like fussy sheep dogs, and the prisoners had that red-eyed, broken-spirited look that prisoners always have. Apart from that nothing much happened that day. There were no newspapers, no bread, no electricity and after a while the water stopped coming through the taps. That night one of the people living in the pension came home and said the two armies had settled their differences and established a modus vivendi. Shortly after that Colonel Kranz suddenly appeared.

Kranz was dressed in a well-cut new uniform, a shade off the regulation U.S. Army khaki. I was surprised to see that he still wore the blue armband of the Liberation Army. He was brisk, light-hearted and exuding charm in the same way and for the same purpose as an octopus squirts ink.

'Alors, David, ça va?' He used to underline his cosmopolitanism by throwing odd sentences in French into his conversation.

'No, I'm afraid it doesn't.'

'Ça ne va pas?' Kranz made a pretence of concern. 'What has happened? Somebody is not treating you properly? Your girl stood you up?'

'No,' I said, 'I'm just fed up.'

'But with what?' Kranz put two thick-fingered paws on my shoulders and did his best to drown me in sympathy. He was a professional cosmopolitan, an actor with a full range of fictitious emotion at his command. He went down well with South Americans. Anglo-Saxons thought they saw through him and, consequently, underrated him.

'Put it this way. I don't appreciate being potted at for no reason that I know of — and without warning, and having to spend the best part of an afternoon hiding in the city's rubbish dumps.'

'You mean the fireworks display? Ah so . . . Well, that was not very amusing, but it was nothing really. These people want to hear a lot of noise. They shoot off their guns in the air like we used to make for New Year's celebration in New York.'

'How many casualties did we have?'

'Twenty-one. It sounded like El Alamein, voyez-vous, et vingt-et-un tués.' He caressed the French words with an awful teutonic intimacy. 'Il y avaient des malentendus, some misunderstandings at a high level. Now everything is smoothed out and things will be fine.'

'Except for the twenty-one who were unlucky,' I said. 'The thing doesn't make sense. Either Balboa is boss or he isn't. If he is, surely he ought to be able to control his army. If he isn't, for God's sake let's get out of it before there are any more misunderstandings at a high level.'

'There will be no more misunderstandings.' Kranz shook his head, lips pursed, the way he did when he wanted you to

33

understand that he had collected some valuable inside information. 'Everything is settled. We have gained our point. The Army of Liberation has been guaranteed a basis of parity with the regular forces.'

'And you know what they can do with it as far as I'm concerned,' I told him.

Kranz overlooked this. He sat down and threw his cap on the bed. I waited, watching out of the corner of my eye for his hand to go up. He had thick black hair in spite of his age, but surprising patches of bare scalp showed through which he always sought to cover with a quick fumble. He was a vain man.

'David,' he said, 'I have some exciting news. The President wants to see you.'

When Kranz said 'President', I knew that he was in. He spoke as if he owned the President, or at least was a member of a syndicate with a good share in him.

'What does he want?' I asked.

'I don't know, but I think it will be something interesting for you.'

'The only proposition Balboa can interest me in at this particular moment is my discharge.'

'You know that's out of the question, David. The President needs you, but to be perfectly frank he thinks it a good plan to reduce the number of Liberation Army officers in the City. He's found a fine job for you to do. You are going to be pleased.'

'No I'm not. I'm going to be bloody angry.'

'How about the finca?' Kranz looked at the ceiling.

'The finca,' I said. 'I don't know. I'm getting to feel that perhaps it's been a sight more bother than it's worth.'

'You'd be out of harm's way wherever the President's sending you, and by the time you got back the commission they've set up would have got down to your case. I'd say it was worth it. It was a good finca, wasn't it? I mean it was worth the fight you've been putting up to get it back?'

'It was a pretty good finca,' I said. 'For its size, anyway. Our family put a lot into it. All the same, I'm beginning to wonder if the whole thing isn't hopeless. Perhaps it's about time I was realistic about it.'

Kranz shook his head in sympathy. 'Well anyway, the audience is for six in the morning. I'm sorry. It's a terrible hour, but the President wants to set an example to his staff. I shall pick you up at five-thirty, and we shall go to the palace together.'

4

At five-thirty Kranz called for me and we walked over to the palace; a building made, I believe, of green soap-stone, with several acres of slippery floors, a staircase ten yards wide, and the biggest chandeliers, so they claimed, in the world. The ferocious, monkey-faced police guarding the palace were the same as ever, and everything was much as it had been, except that as the electricity had not yet been switched on the rooms were lit with oil lamps, and the por-traits of Werner, handsome and frowning in three-quarters profile, had gone.

General Balboa had made a gesture of declining to occupy the presidential suite, and had chosen for his office one of the ante-rooms previously occupied by an under-secretary. The office was at the end of a corridor of polished tiles, and we picked our way across this like mountaineers on a glacier. We were shown into the Presence on the stroke of six. General Dionisio Balboa was seated at a small table under a vast, dusty chandelier, and the room's sole other occupant was a middle-aged female secretary with a purple birthmark over one cheek. There were several calendars on the walls, each having the thirteenth day of the month blanked out by a small picture of a saint.

The President got up and came from behind the table and Kranz clicked his heels in a way that sent a slight shudder through his body. 'Your Excellency — Captain Williams.'

'Enchanted,' Balboa said, without warmth. I got a quick, hard handshake and a smile that seemed to be checked before it could develop. He waved towards two cane-seated office chairs placed beside his desk, and we sat down.

Balboa came as a surprise. In this country physical bulk is evidence of success, and I had pictured the General as thick-set, genial and expansive in the tradition of Latin-American dictators; like a Porfirio Diaz, without the moustaches. But President Balboa was small and thin, modest in his manner, even nervous. Looking at him, I could imagine the change that would come over him in the next ten years — if he lived as long as that.

'So this is the officer you were telling me about, Colonel Kranz,' Balboa said in English, forcing another smile.

'Yes, your Excellency.'

'Splendid,' Balboa said, successfully extracting any trace of enthusiasm from the word. He gave me a prolonged stare. 'Do you speak Spanish, Captain Williams?'

'I do, sir.' I noted the sudden promotion was confirmed.

'Then I wonder if it would disturb you if we conducted our conversation in that language? This would relieve me of feeling a linguistic inferiority.' Again the checked smile.

'Captain Williams has spent fourteen years in the country,' Kranz said. I felt that I should have broken in to explain that most of these fourteen years had been passed in my childhood.

Balboa nodded. 'Mostly at Istapa, I believe.' He had a good memory, it seemed, and he liked to show it off.

'Captain Williams,' Balboa said, 'we need an officer to conduct an operation in the provinces — one who is resolute but also capable, above all, of restraint. Colonel Kranz has put forward your name, and has recommended you because you are familiar with the district and also because you possess a quality which is rather rare among our people — that of tact. Have you informed Captain Williams of the nature of

37

the mission, Colonel Kranz?' His eyes swivelled suddenly in Kranz's direction and I was reminded of the quick sideways scramble of small, black crabs.

'No, sir.'

General Balboa's expression had saddened. 'There is a certain amount of unrest among the Indians at the moment in various parts of the country. This is natural and to be expected. The propaganda of the last régime had a good deal of success among the Indians.'

Balboa looked at me and then at Kranz. He waited and Kranz said: 'The Indians are like children.'

The President nodded his acceptance of the contribution. 'As we all know, Werner gave the Indians land. If Werner did not like you he took your land away and gave it to the Indians. None of us are going to believe that he did this because of his great paternal love for the Indians.' The President gave a sudden and startling screech of laughter, which transformed itself into a tinkle in the enormous chandelier. 'No. He wanted to secure their support for his criminal policies. And what did the Indians do with this great gift of land that suddenly fell from the skies? That also we know. They cut down the coffee and banana plantations growing on it, and then proceeded to dedicate a little corner of it — perhaps one-tenth, let us say — to the production of maize and beans which they ate themselves and which is all they require from life. The rest of the land? That, of course, was allowed to return to the bush. What do you call that? Land reform? Agrarian suicide?'

'The act of a criminal maniac,' Kranz said. 'Un fou dangereux.'

'So much for land reform,' Balboa said. 'And now, we may ask, was any attempt ever made to raise these poor abandoned people to our level?'

I felt the President's hard gaze upon me and felt obliged to shake my head.

'No. They were left to live and die like pigs. They were denied all the aspirations which it is the duty of the State to foster in the humblest of its subjects.'

I noted that Balboa had the true leader's gift for making a platitude sound like a newly discovered truth.

'We are going to put the last government's policy into reverse,' Balboa said. 'The Indian will be integrated into the life of the nation, and some very interesting experiments in this direction are already under way.'

'The expropriated land, sir, is to be returned to its previous owners, I'm given to understand,' Kranz said.

'Yes. That is so. It has now been proved that to leave the Indian to his own devices is to allow him to sink back into the Stone Age. This cannot be tolerated in a modern State. The Indian will be guided upwards — if necessary, despite himself. We shall meet with resistance, that is certain. And such opposition, wherever it arises, must be countered and overcome with firmness, but also with patience. We must always remember that it is not the Indian who is to blame, but the unscrupulous agitator who has exploited him.' Balboa sighed. 'There must be no bloodshed.'

I believe he meant it. In half a century Central America had seen a hundred revolutions, and I supposed that a fair percentage of the men who had come to power as a result of them had started off as reformers. For a year or two they had disdained to line their pockets, and refused to allow their supporters to line theirs. Sometimes it was a simple case of frustrated greed that drove the supporters to revolt and thus start the killing. At first the new man killed to preserve justice, and then after a short time out of mere suspicion, till in the end he became like a mangy old tiger, feared and detested by all who surrounded him, ruling by the torture chamber and the secret police.

'We need cool heads,' Balboa said, 'a firm hand and much sympathy. There are a dozen places where a delicate situation has arisen and each one presents a different problem. There is also a very great shortage of just men. You know the Chilams of Guadaloupe, don't you, Captain?'

'No, sir, I don't. Most of the peones at our Soledad finca were recruited from them, but we never got to know anything about them. They came and worked off their debts and then they went back to the mountains. Our only contact with them was through the caporales.'

'You are quite right. They are a mysterious people. All our Indians are mysterious. We know little more of their lives than our ancestors did when they first came to this country. At all events, Captain, I want you to go to Guadaloupe as soon as possible and take control of the situation there. I should like you to leave not later than tomorrow.'

Up to this point I had been quite unshakeable in my determination not to be involved in further Central American adventures, or in any extension of the present one, and I have never been able to understand how it was that Balboa succeeded in undermining this determination in an interview lasting not much more than half an hour. He was a man with a charm which flashed out at you, all the more surprisingly after the initial impression he gave of coldness, and he had an indefinable quality, usually described as personal magnetism, that was greater than the charm. Balboa never said anything that was striking, or novel, or in any way profound. Analysing it all in retrospect I came to the conclusion that he had nothing more than a stock of politician's arguments, but coming from Balboa they carried conviction — at least temporarily.

Only one thought seemed to trouble his quiet, sincere confidence. How could he ask me or anyone else to leave Guatemala City, and even in the interests of the Cause, to bury themselves in a place like Guadaloupe? 'Here you are alive. You have the feeling of being in the centre of things.

40

But Guadaloupe is so very quiet. Really it is not an exciting place.'

The President meant it, as he meant everything he said. He was a man totally lacking in a sense of humour.

5

I DID not sleep well that night. The massacre at the river seemed to have affected me badly, producing ever since a regular crop of nightmares which at their worst woke me every few minutes. I came to the conclusion that despite my experiences in the Second World War I could never before have known horror or fear in an extreme form. Indeed, I discovered that although I had seen many battlefields strewn with corpses, I had never — until the slaughter in the jungle — seen death by violence.

The fact was that in our modern wars we didn't think of ourselves as blowing people to bits, burning them in their tanks, burying them alive under the buildings where they sheltered. We laid fire by map references and calculations, and by the time we arrived on the scene of our operations what was present in the way of human detritus was quite impersonal; a matter of waxwork figures — part of the accepted furniture of battlefields. We modern warriors felt a mathematician's detachment and isolation from the macabre unreality of these landscapes we produced. But this sudden contact with the basic facts of war had struck deep into my being, and a great number of horrific details of the slaughter which I had contrived to forget in my waking hours were nightly displayed to me in these recurrent dreams.

The massacre was always mixed up in some way with the finca — which was to be expected because the finca was the background for all my dreams. All my dreams were arranged around the stage scenery and properties provided by the old house, the narrow valley under the volcanoes, and a mute chorus of the Indian peones who worked in the plantations. All the events of the last fifteen years had to be distorted, stretched or compressed until they fitted into this emotional dreamscape. And in these recent nightmares my grandfather was there as ever, slightly contemptuous of me, majestically untouched by the violence and the flowing of blood; and so was my father there — but, ineffectual and horrified, he offered no protection. Greta also appeared. Tragedy was enough to call her back into my dreams, although in these days I contrived to think of her so rarely.

I got up well before dawn, took a taxi and went through the paling night down to the station. By the time the sun was up we were already rattling out of Guatemala City on the Guadaloupe train.

The town's coloured suburbs were quickly soaked up in jungle as we began the slow descent to the lowlands. For four hours the train crawled down into the country's sweltering depths. Then for four hours it climbed again, flipping jerkily through the pages of a tropical sketch book: a glimpse of a volcano's scalded cone with a rag of cloud at its apex; a half-circle of humble men in aprons, knee-length trousers and felt hats waiting by the tracks as if for a recurrent miracle; huge rocks squatting on eroded buttocks at the edge of the jungle; fat-fleshed, thirsty vegetation sprouting in dry places; a boy with a black, tail-whipping snake held in a cleft stick; a few silent, cautious villages plaited out of dirty straw. Most of the passengers were Indians. They sat in the twelve oblong box-like compartments, wedged in position by their knees and sadly attentive to the details of the journey. Whenever the train jolted to a standstill or jerked forward again, their hats fell off and they seized them and clamped them back on

43

their heads. They were men with mournful eyes and the moustaches of Chinese sages, and all their women held silent babies to their copious, blue-veined breasts. Whenever they spoke to each other they did so in a quick secret mumble without turning their heads.

A journalist called Hernandez was travelling down with me to report on the situation. He was a young man with a fine, almost noble expression who had started life as a motor-mechanic and was going to be a politician. Hernandez had worked in a garage in Brownsville, Texas. When he had gathered a comfortable fortune in politics he was going to emigrate to Miami and spend the rest of his days there. I asked him what attracted him about Miami but he did not appear to understand the question. You no more asked questions about Miami now than you would have about the Kingdom of Heaven in the old days. Hernandez carried a thermos flask full of Coca-Cola which most generously he offered to share and a Spanish language edition of *Reader's Digest*. In the gaps in our conversation he read it slowly, underlining some of the passages.

It turned out that in the thirty years of his life Hernandez had never before left the capital except to go to Brownsville. He had got hold of some nasty rumours about what had been happening in Guadaloupe and this had made him nervous and depressed. What he liked to do was to go to the movies and he had organized his life to give himself the maximum time enjoying what the cinema had to show him of the world. His work at the office started at seven-thirty every morning, and he finished at one. This gave him the chance to visit a cinema twice a day, and he had done so with occasional days off for sickness for the last five years. Hernandez saw all the films that came to Guatemala, and he saw the big hits two or three times. When the cinemas closed at night he went and sat in a soda-fountain over a milk-shake until that closed too, and then he went to bed. This was his life, and he had created of it a reality of its own, and to leave it now for a new arrangement of facts presented to him by the Guatemala hinterland was to face something that was nightmarish and lacking in solidity.

Hernandez told me this in between his dippings into *Reader's Digest*, his possession of which stamped him as an intellectual by Central American standards. He was too restless and nervous to concentrate for long upon his reading.

'You ever been in the Lux on Sixth Avenue?'

'I think so,' I said. 'Most probably. That's the one opposite the Capitol, isn't it?'

'Not opposite. It's half a block down the street.' Hernandez smiled slightly at a memory. 'You can get out of the first evening performance at the Lux and make the Capitol in time for the second house. If you have to go over to one of the other places like the Roxy or the Rex it means you lose most of a short. Why I mentioned the Lux was because they give more leg-room. It's kind of more comfortable the way they fixed it up.' Hernandez gazed down at his knees, trapped between those of the two Indians sitting opposite.

'Of course, the Variadades is a good bit cheaper, but you don't get the comfort, and they really cut into the programme with the advertising they put on in that dump.'

The Indian woman squeezed in next to Hernandez cupped her hands under her baby's mouth, and the baby puked softly into them. Hernandez looked quickly away out of the window only to be faced with the unreality of cactus and volcano. He hastily rejected the sight.

He wanted to know what we could expect of Guadaloupe, and I told him. It was one of those run-down towns with a history but with no cinema, absolutely no soda-fountain or Turf Club, no Sunday concert in the plaza, no special time set aside for the upper-class routine evening promenade — in fact, a ghost town as far as he was concerned. Then I remembered the hotels.

45

'There are five or six hotels,' I told him.

'Decent places with American Bars and all that?'

'I suppose so. Yes, they've got American Bars. Most of them. But they'll all be empty now. Probably closed down, too.' He saddened again. 'The foreign planters kept them going,' I explained, 'and now they've gone they could never keep their heads above water. They'll have put up the shutters by now. You can always get a drink in a cantina, but they're pretty tough. We used to keep out of them. Too many gun-fights from an ordinary holiday-maker's point of view.'

That was a fair enough outline of Guadaloupe and its possibilities, I thought. It was the only part that would be likely to interest Hernandez, and I omitted to mention that the planters used to go there in the hot season for its climate, and for the lake which was only an hour's ride away and was reckoned as one of the beauty spots of Central America. Guadaloupe was at an altitude of nearly seven thousand feet. It had this wonderful sparkling climate all the year round, and the countryside was beautiful, but in an unearthly way, and very sad and silent. Everybody who visited Guadaloupe for the first time always wanted to settle there, but nobody ever did, and they never succeeded in turning it into a Guatemalan Matlock Spa. The Indians weren't picturesque either. I tried to think of something that might recommend the place to Hernandez and I remembered the church. 'There's a church,' I said, 'if you're interested. It's rather outside my line, but people who go in for Baroque architecture say there's something special about it. I'm afraid I couldn't tell you what it is.'

'At least they're Christians,' Hernandez said.

'Well, no,' I said. 'That is, not the Indians. They may have been nominally until forty or fifty years ago, and then they kicked their priests out and took over. The whites don't go into the church now. The Indians do their costumbres

46

there and the whites don't like it. The Indians don't like to have whites about the place either. When I was there a few years ago a chap got slashed for taking photographs of them while they were doing whatever it is they do. It's better to keep away from them.'

Hernandez put down his book and thought about this. 'It doesn't sound much of a place, does it?' he said.

6

WE got into Guadaloupe in the late afternoon. The hotels I inquired about were closed so, leaving Hernandez, who had a letter to friends of his family, I went to a rather sad side-street pension I remembered from the old days, took a room and cleaned myself up. Afterwards I had a drink, and then I went down to have a look at the town.

At first I thought Guadaloupe hadn't changed, and there were none of the signs that one gets to recognize of trouble of any kind. The shops of the ladinos were all open for business. It was quiet where I expected it to be quiet, and also very noisy where I expected it to be noisy, and people were going about doing roughly the same things that, from my experience, they always did at this time of day.

The thing to remember about Guadaloupe was that it was a ladino town. There are one or two places in Guatemala, like the City itself, which are accepted as being 'white', and there are many pure Indian villages in the mountains; but most of the small towns like Guadaloupe are peopled by ladinos, who are a strong and recent mixture of the two races. The ladinos on the whole are dark and striking. They are a people who dress in Western fashions as well as they can afford, who like to ride rather than walk, to work without soiling the hands, to promenade at set hours and in the proper places, to marry their daughters well, to dabble in politics and accumulate money. An infinite distance separates them from the Indian side of their ancestry.

The ladinos of Guadaloupe live unheedingly among grandiose vestiges of the past. It is a town of majestic ruin, cracked splendour and tarnished gilt. The old stone houses are blind-walled, with rare windows defended by massive grilles and enormous doorways through which a man could ride without dismounting from his horse. The main square known as the plaza is enclosed by superb colonial buildings, including a church like a cathedral. There are other streets and squares, but the streets are narrow and ill-paved, and the squares are hidden among decaying buildings decorated with the stone escutcheons of extinct nobility.

There are also shops, and drinking dives called cantinas, all of them single-storeyed and painted in fierce colours. The fronts of the shops are painted with pictures which dramatize the goods sold inside: a bull charges at you head down and nostrils distended from the façade of the butchers, and the front of the cantina called 'The Noble Visitor' shows an American in a big hat being served with a whisky while seated in his jeep. The church in the square is the one where the Indians got rid of their priest. That was in the days when there were more Indians than ladinos in Guadaloupe. Its exterior is wrapped in coils of a soft yellow stone and it has a square belfry, badly cracked by several earthquakes, and containing a large green bell.

It was about eight o'clock when I got to the plaza. The sun had set, and the shopkeepers and their wives, with their children and their Indian servants dressed up in ribbons and flounced skirts like souvenir dolls, were going round the square in the before-dinner promenade. They were all going in the same direction round three sides of the square and then at a certain point turning all together and walking back again, like a watch movement oscillating on a pivot, which in this case happened to be a monument to Liberty.

There was a tremendous familiar din coming out of the open doors of the two cantinas 'My Bet' and 'Thou and I', which are both round the corner from the plaza and are practically shrines built to house powerful juke-boxes that play at all times when the electricity is not cut off. I walked up and down the main street twice under the cool, brilliant blue-green of the sky before I realized what it was that had changed about the place. The Indians had practically disappeared. Someone had cleared away all the straw and adobe shacks and cleaned up the town. The Indians you used to see all along the street, lying wrapped in their blankets in the angle of the wall, had gone. They had got rid of the shrinking, drunken, taciturn Indians at last, and the only place where I saw a few of them was on the steps of the church, where before going in they were swinging censers and praying in loud, conversational tones to their gods.

The change that had come about since I had last been in Guadaloupe, about five years before, only exemplified a process that had been going on for centuries — although here it seemed to have been greatly speeded up. The Indian is vanishing. He is withdrawing himself silently, dying out or being changed into a ladino.

There are tenacious, encircled Indian communities holding out everywhere, but their numbers are always getting less, and there are more and more ladinos being born. The Indian is like a man in a hypnotic sleep, carrying out with a kind of blind unreason the commands laid upon him by priests and chieftains who died over four hundred years ago. The commands may no longer mean anything, but the Indian carries them out. His life takes shape round the core of an empty, meaningless secret, which has only one purpose — to keep him an Indian. He can never change, but slowly the ladino, who is a true product of the times, supplants him. The ladino has no past. No voices speak to him from the dead. He is perfectly adjusted to this century and he

50

marches forward towards the brightest of futures, of the kind which includes detached villas and two cars in the garage.

A starvation diet and the seduction of their daughters had foredoomed the Indians in Guadaloupe — evolutionary factors, inexorable but slow. Yet the Indians had gone. Within only five years, as a racial group, they had disappeared. Whatever accelerated catastrophe had intervened, Guadaloupe now swarmed with trim ladinos who dressed like whites, lived like whites, and in fact could have passed for whites but for the colour of their skins, which are better adjusted to the realities of the climate.

The passing of the Indian, apart from the little stubborn party of worshippers at the church, had perhaps improved the aspect of the place from a white man's point of view. The ladino is a cheerful and sociable being. He is forward-looking, imitative and anxious to please, and all these things the Indian is not.

Workmen were hanging up a picture of the President in the town hall when I got there. It was the first I had seen of him, and it was rather blurred, as if it had been reproduced in a hurry from an old passport photograph. If anything, this picture exaggerated the President's deceptively mild and almost apologetic expression. 'Freedom — Justice — Balboa!' it said underneath the portrait. The workmen had hung it over the dark, unfaded patch of wall where Werner's picture had hung before. Werner's picture had been larger than the new portrait so that a wide border of dark green paint showed behind it against the faded nondescript of the wall.

There was nobody about but the men hanging up the picture. I wandered down passages and looked into empty room after room. I was looking for the mayor — or intendente as he is called locally. At last I found a man sitting at a desk heaped up with dog-eared papers. He had one shoe off and was hitting at a nail in its sole with the edge of a heavy rubber stamp. I stood there in the doorway, and he went on hammering at the shoe. This man was dressed in the thick, black respectability of a ladino municipal employee, but I was surprised to see that he was an Indian. The electric current in the weak lamp hanging over his head was coming and going like a pulse, but I was sure that I caught a glance from under his eyebrows. He put the shoe down, felt inside it, and picked up the rubber stamp again. 'I'm looking for the intendente,' I said in a loud voice. 'Is he still here?' It was part of my background that I could always get an authoritarian ring into my voice when I was talking to Indians.

The man put the shoe down and felt inside it again. 'I'm the intendente.' He did not look up. 'Who are you?'

This coming from an Indian, even if he happened to represent the civil authority, really startled me. It was a fantastic piece of bluntness for this part of the world. I told him that I was the new military commander for the area, but the news did not galvanize him. 'I call myself Miguel,' he said. Not even Miguel-at-your-service, which any ladino and almost any Indian would have said.

He took the envelope I gave him containing my credentials and pushed it into the heap of papers in front of him, and I saw his hand reaching out for the shoe again. 'Be so kind as to give me your attention,' I said as severely as I could. I cuffed some papers off the seat of the only available chair and sat down.

The intendente took the shoe resolutely and jiggled with it. His eyes were at the level of my belt. He had the broadest head I had ever seen, and a bronze idol's face with polished cheek bones and insignificant eyes. Behind him on the wall there was a propaganda poster showing a naked corpse with the grotesquely swollen testicles of a man who has been strung up by the private parts. 'A Victim of a Godless

Régime', it said, but I was almost certain that I had seen the same picture before, about the time when the government before the last fell — the everlasting anonymous victim of Central American politics.

'I want to get from you your own story of what actually has been happening here,' I said.

The intendente dropped the shoe and his hand went with a quick, sly movement into the heap of paper. 'I have submitted a report. If you wish to see a copy, it is here.' He was holding a small scroll tied with black tape.

'Thank you,' I said, 'I am grateful. But I've come for the unofficial account, not the official one. Oblige me by beginning at the beginning.'

'The beginning? I've got a bad memory. It only goes back forty years.' The intendente gave me a quick, stubborn glance.

'We'll start with what happened after the liberation. That will be two months and will do for the present.'

'The liberation? Well, it's quite simple. The liberation took place, and shortly afterwards the order came for the Indians to give up the land.'

'The land they had taken over illegally?'

'No, the land they took over legally, after the government passed the law giving the Indians one-fifth of property previously owned by the Company.'

'The Universal Coffee Company?'

'Yes, of course. The Universal Coffee Company.'

'Wait a minute,' I said. 'Wasn't there a stopgap measure by the President, permitting the Indians to remain in possession of land actually awarded them by the last government?'

'Whatever the President's measure permitted, the land was taken back. The Company police came and turned the Indians out.'

'And was there any disturbance — resistance of any kind?'

'Why should there be? They gave the Indians land and

53

then they took it back. The Indians lost nothing. Why should they resist?'

'And then the police burned the crops?'

'They burned only part of the crops. The beans would not burn. After they burned the maize they drove teams of oxen over the fields to spoil the beans.'

'So then the trouble started?'

'No. There was no trouble then. After the Company police had burned the Indians' houses and destroyed their crops, the Indians wished to go to the mountains, but later the police collected all the people to take them all to the Company's barracks.'

'And what was the idea of that?'

'So that they would work for the Company. In my report I said that some of the Indian young men would not go to the Company's barracks with the police. They escaped and went to the mountains.'

At this point I got the impression that the intendente had no more to say. I suddenly felt relieved. Probably no one had troubled to read right through his report, any more than they had troubled to show it to me. 'Well, what's all the fuss about?' I asked him. After all, who cared whether U.C.'s slave-labour succeeded in making a break for it or not? Good luck to them if they did. I had no sympathy to waste on U.C. Even if Werner hadn't ruined the small planters when he did, U.C. would have done so in the end. To hell with U.C.! They could look after themselves.

The intendente was examining his shoe again. He had succeeded in half-forgetting me. I was slightly surprised when he spoke, sounding this time as if he was talking to himself. 'After the young men went they came back at night and broke into the town armoury. There are thirteen rifles missing.'

My heart sank, but I still refused to be stripped so easily of my conviction that any trouble that might be brewing here could be settled by negotiation. 'They probably wanted the guns to hunt with,' I suggested.

'Yes, to hunt men when the time comes,' the intendente said. 'They have become bandits. After a while they will be caught, and when they are caught they will be shot.'

'Or it could be that they will spend a few months apiece in prison.'

'The prisons are full. It is more convenient to shoot them.'

'There are such things as trials.'

'Perhaps they will give them a trial. Perhaps not. What does it matter?'

The intendente really didn't care one way or the other, I thought. In secret he might have been proud of his race, but the fate of individuals was of absolutely no importance. These semi-pagans made far less distinction than we did between the living and the dead. Life was not particularly sweet to them, and although death was to be avoided if possible, it hadn't the terror it held for most self-supposed Christians. Life was really cheap among the Indians. I was probably more worried about the fate of the thirteen men than the intendente was.

The square was lit up for the after-dinner promenade, and the whole town was gathering there. The noise of the chatter, the giggling and the shouting, with the distant juke-box music mixed in, became terrific. Every now and then a policeman on a motor cycle would charge round the square and a fan of light from his headlamp would open and close across the ceiling.

'Who's going to shoot them without trial?' I shouted above the clatter of the engine.

The intendente didn't reply. He looked amused.

'Do you mean to suggest that I am?'

'You will do as you please. You may be sure that my services in my official capacity are at your disposal.'

'Splendid,' I said, taking a chance. 'In that case I will

55

rely on you to establish contact with these thirteen men and assure them that if the rifles are surrendered immediately, and no crime has been committed, they will receive the President's pardon.'

'And the Company?'

'What about the Company?'

'The Company does not give pardons, and the President is in Guatemala City.'

'Tell the men to surrender, and I'll take care of the Company. I give my word that if the arms are handed over the Indians will be given free choice as to whether they work for the Company or not. It depends now upon you. Can you find a way of communicating with the men?'

'I do not know, and if I can, it will be of no use.'

'Why are you so sure?'

He waited while the motor cycle went by again. Then he answered.

'These promises have been made to their fathers and their grandfathers, and they believed them. And what happened?' He half turned in his chair and nodded towards the picture of the corpse with the swollen genitals. 'They are stupid people, but in the end they learn their lesson.'

———————

7

I CAME up against the Company next day in the person of its Central American manager, Winthrop Elliot. Hernandez had finished his report, which he said was on the whole optimistic, but his editor wanted him to interview the celebrated Elliot before he went back and to persuade Elliot to show him over the U.C.'s 'Chilam Project', which had been given a lot of publicity in the City — some of it unfavourable.

Elliot invited us both to lunch at the Mayapan. This was the newest in Guatemalan luxury hotels. It had been built out of the ruins of a seventeenth-century convent, and the dining-room, where we were the only guests, was called the Refectory. Meeting Elliot, I found that my imagination had let me down. I had pictured this man as a cigar-chewing tycoon, but he turned out to be small, quick and cat-like, fiftyish, with a forehead like a strip-cartoon professor. Elliot somehow gave you an anatomical sensation. You were conscious all the time of the bones straining the stretched skin, and the veins on the back of his hands looked as though they had been injected with blue dye for the benefit of medical students. He was strangely mild in expression and manner, and just as people sometimes appear to look through you, Elliot smiled through you, gently.

He crooked his finger and three fantastically dressed Indians emerged from a background of cloisters, dodged round a fountain and gained our table. Elliot studied the menu. 'Now that looks like a very attractive choice to me. What do you gentlemen feel like? Personally I'm going to make it a ham steak, Waikiki style, but don't let me influence you.'

We ordered ham steaks, too, and Elliot recommended candied yams and tossed green salad as an accompaniment. 'And right now, Mr Hernandez — before we go any further — I want to thank you for coming along. Thank you, too, Captain Williams. It's a pleasure to know both you gentlemen.'

Hernandez and I agreed that it was a pleasure to know Elliot as well, and Hernandez tried to make a start with his interview. 'Mr Elliot — I don't quite know how to put this — but the fact is — as you have heard — that public opinion in the City is a little uneasy about the Indian situation up here.'

'What exactly do you mean by the Indian *situation*, Mr Hernandez?'

'Well, I guess you might say certain problems that are supposed to have arisen.' Hernandez was trying to respond to Elliot's unvarying slight smile, which was rather like that of a head-mistress dealing with a none-too-bright child. Hernandez's own smile had become fixed and embarrassed.

'You don't by any chance mean problems arising out of my company's Chilam Indian Project, do you?' Elliot asked benignly.

'It's more a matter of rumour,' Hernandez said. 'Naturally I don't pay any attention to them personally, but there are a lot of rumours floating about.'

'This much I can assure you — there are no difficulties down at the Project.' Elliot still managed to look indulgent. 'We stopped having problems when friend Werner took off. All the Indian needs is the right kind of guidance, and we're doing our best to give it to him. That's all any of us can do, isn't it — our best?'

58

'You're absolutely right there, sir.'

'Fine. And now I suggest that the most satisfactory solution for all concerned is for you two gentlemen to come along as soon as possible and see for yourselves how things are working out. Come when you like, stay as long as you like, ask all the questions you like. I'm sure you'll agree that that's the only way to form an unbiased opinion. Am I correct?'

We agreed that this was the best thing to do just as the waiters materialized silently with the sweet course. For the first time I took in the details of their remarkable costume, which included a shirt woven with animal designs, a kind of leather kilt, and a short, red cape. Elliot noticed my interest. 'We had an authentic historian at work on that outfit. They tell me it's the nearest we can get to what these people were wearing when Cortes showed up. I'd appreciate having your opinion on it.'

'It's remarkable,' I told him.

'Reminds me of a movie they showed in the City last year,' Hernandez said. 'It was based on the Bible. I shall remember the title in a minute.'

Elliot nodded at each of us in turn. 'Well, the way I see it, it's at least more pleasing to the eye than the garb they were going around in before we took over.'

'Does your company actually own the Mayapan then, Mr Elliot?' Hernandez asked.

'It owns all the hotels in this town,' Elliot said. 'I know people usually assume we're only interested in coffee, but actually we dabble in all kinds of things. That's where we have it over United Fruit. The tourist industry's only the latest of our babies — and, by the way, it happens to be our opinion that it's going to be *the* Central American industry of the future. As you would have expected, Werner nearly put paid to it in Guatemala, but now things have been straightened out again we're all set to go ahead. I have a hunch that in a month's time there won't be an hotel room to be had in this town without prior reservation.'

Hernandez began to write in his book. 'That's very interesting. Now do you have some kind of regular programme fixed up?'

'We most certainly do. The way we see it is that this is a potential tourist paradise. It has everything — climate, wonderful scenic attractions, and a very romantic past. What we figure is that all we have to do is to encourage people to come and see the place for themselves, and they're bound to be sold on it. We plan to organize a big-scale fiesta to coincide with the Indian New Year in just under a month's time. We have chartered Skymasters flying in from New Orleans and a boat-load of visitors coming up by train from Puerto Barrios. About half this first bunch are executives of travel organizations and publicity men we've invited along to see how things are shaping up. While we're on the subject, Mr Hernandez, I'd like on behalf of the company to extend an invitation to you and to your Editor — if if he can get away from his desk. Naturally you'd be our guests for the occasion.'

'Thank you, Mr Elliot. I'll certainly convey your invitation to Mr Rossi — although I expect you know what it is. I know Mr Rossi will be most appreciative.'

'I don't want to burden you with details, but if it's likely to be of any interest to your readers we're planning at present to organize seven and fourteen-day all-in tours. For the sake of convenience we call them our Regular and our De Luxe Pioneer-Caravans. We aim to offer our guests plenty of excitement and all the adventure they can handle. We're going to take them up to the tops of volcanoes where — as you know — the Indians still perform their colourful rites; give them a run in a powerful motor launch on Lake Tenyuchin — and by the way, we've learned from an old Indian legend that the lake is supposed to be haunted and — as you might suppose — we're playing up this theme in our promotion literature.' Elliot laughed genially. 'And then, of course, we've some wonderful old ruins to show them with a hidden-treasure angle. For those who feel like it we have specially equipped and air-conditioned ranch-wagons for a hunting trip down to the jungle, with every chance to get a shot at a jaguar in perfect safety. We're planning to make a great speciality of serving native foods, prepared under proper hygienic conditions. Adventurous Dining, we call it. They all go in for adventure these days. Have you seen those 'Get Lost and Like It' ads put out by the Key Biscoyne Hotels group? That's what I call pretty smart psychology.'

Hernandez, who could only understand people wanting to get lost in Guatemala City, did his best to agree.

'That's only a beginning,' Elliot said. 'The really big stuff, like the Lost-City Helicopter Hunts and the Dome-Liner observation cars on the railway, comes later. What we're concentrating on right now is basic local colour, and we're doing a thorough job from the ground up. For example, when people come to see an Indian place they expect it to look like one, so to start with we're building a complete typical Indian village right from the word go.

'What happened to the original Indian village?' I asked, beginning at last to see the daylight.

'We tore it down. There's a difference between a place being picturesque and being a plain eyesore. All the workers living on our project outside the town have ideal housing conditions and they're dressed like sensible human beings, but that isn't what tourists want to see. They want to see a typical native family with the woman suckling the kid and her man busy at his craft, whatever it is. To give you some idea of the lengths we've gone to, we actually flew in our silver-workers from Mexico.'

'Am I to understand we don't have native silver-workers in Guatemala, sir?' Hernandez said, still writing in his book.

'Not that I know of, and so far as this immediate locality goes there isn't a single thing they turn out that's worth looking at. We're fixing up a native market for visitors, and every article they're going to be interested to buy — baskets, ponchos, pottery and — well — interesting souvenirs in general, will have to be brought in from some place else — mostly Mexico. Imagine that.'

'How about colourful native ceremonies, or maybe dances?' Hernandez asked. 'Couldn't the town elders arrange to put on a dance for you?'

'They don't exist. There aren't any. The only thing they do here when they put on a fiesta is to walk round the streets carrying a black box like a coffin and then get drunk. We've had to ask the mayor to use his influence to put a stop to it. If any tourist gets his camera out they spit at him. That kind of thing isn't box office.'

Trying to avoid any suggestion of sarcasm I asked Elliot whether he thought there was any chance of educating the local Chilams up to a tourist standard of picturesqueness, and he took the question seriously.

'Well now, that happens to be just what we have in mind. The way things are now ninety-five per cent of Project labour works in the plantations and the mines, but we've started a scheme by which any worker with a good enough I.Q. who looks like he wants to do something for himself, has a chance to earn promotion to the tourist side. If we can replace the people we have to bring in by local labour — well, that's fine. It's going to save U.C. a lot of money, if it can be done. In the meanwhile, let's face it, this has to be strictly comic opera. It's not an ideal solution, but it's the best that can be done with the material on hand. And then again I suppose we have to remember that people on vacation are like a lot of kids who want to believe in fairy tales.'

After lunch Elliot took us over to see the celebrated Chilam

Project. We drove at a steady eighty miles per hour down five miles of the finest asphalted highway in Central America. A specially installed radio calling itself the Golden Throat System filled the ranch-wagon with high-fidelity pop music, and a cool breeze, slightly perfumed with the odour of pine-wood, was fanned about our ears. Elliot had hardly begun to tell us about the unusual features of this car when we pulled up at a gate in a high wire fence. At the soft braying of the horn a man came out of a sentry box and let us in. We stopped just inside the gate and Elliot opened the door and skipped down from the car, Hernandez and I following. We found ourselves at the top of a gentle slope, and below us was laid out a miniature town. It was stark white, as regular as a military cemetery, and as unreal as stage scenery or a scale model produced as a Christmas attraction by a departmental store. From where we stood we looked straight down a street lined with white box-like cabins, each with a door and single window, and surrounded by a low, spiked fence. Young shade trees, all the same size and shape, had been planted at equal intervals. The street ended in a square with a clock tower in its centre, which dominated the whole town. The clock tower looked as if it had been carefully painted on the very symmetrical mountain at the end of the valley. 'This is Fifth Avenue,' Elliot said, 'and that's Times Square at the bottom. Suppose we take a walk down there.'

A group of Indians carrying metal sprayers fed from tanks strapped on their backs hurried past. They were dressed in grey denim pyjamas and were a little hunched, as if walking through a low tunnel. Elliot grinned benevolently. 'There goes a squad from the K.P. roster. Their job is to go round disinfecting the chalets every day. Of course all the regular personnel are down at the plantations right now, so the town is going to look kind of empty. Mr Hernandez — please fire away with any questions that may occur to you.'

Hernandez hesitated, taken perhaps by surprise at this

sudden demand for intelligent interest, and Elliot waited with a trace of gentle impatience. 'Perhaps I may be allowed to throw in a suggestion for one or two facts your readers might care to know about. For instance, I feel that many of them would be glad to read an official denial that any element of compulsion or duress enters into our scheme of things. Each and every man and woman in this Project has asked to come in. To be accurate, ninety-one per cent of the Chilam tribe have contracted in legal form to enter the scheme for a minimum trial period of five years. Every adult has voluntarily affixed his mark to the form of contract in the presence of a public notary. I repeat that every Indian was treated as a free agent.' Elliot's tone was coloured slightly with the reverence which big-scale industrialists and merchants give the impression of feeling about their enterprises.

We stopped for a moment, squeezed into the small ragged pool of shade under one of the trees, while Hernandez got these facts into his book. It was much hotter here than in Guadaloupe because the Company town had been built at a lower altitude, midway between the coffee fincas in the mountains and the banana plantations down in the tropics. The light was brilliant and yet soft, and the unreal, white cabins sparkled against the deep, misted blue of the mountains.

'Got that down, Mr Hernandez?' Elliot asked. 'Good. It occurs to me, by the way, that you might care to have me go over what you've written before submitting it to your Editor. I make the suggestion because you strike me as a man with a great respect for accuracy. Naturally, I leave it to you — but I'll be glad to help if I can. Now here's another interesting fact which ought to explode a few of the popular misconceptions that seem to have been floating around. The Project does not — repeat not — pay its workers wages in cash. They do, however, receive in credit value approximately twice the wages paid by independent planters. U.C. has

64

thrown overboard the old pernicious system so long favoured by the planters of keeping workers permanently in debt so as to secure their labour. All members of our work force are at all times in credit with the Company. Got all that? . . . Fine. Now, let's take a quick peek at a family chalet before we move on.'

We trooped into a family chalet, stooping a little as we passed through the doorway. It consisted of a single starkly painted room, about twelve feet by eight, with a small deal table, two low chairs, a simple bedstead with a blanket folded army-style, a mosquito-net hanging from a peg above, and a decorated mirror on the wall. A faint chemical sourness neutered the atmosphere. 'Hygiene and order,' Elliot said happily, 'are the first steps towards civilization. Each chalet has its own outside toilet and there's a wash-place with a piped water supply between every four families. Notice that the K.P.s have just been through for the morning disinfection.' Elliot took several photographs out of his pocket. 'And now having seen something of what we've done here about housing, you gentlemen might care to refresh your memory by taking a look at these pictures of the old Indian village up at Guadaloupe before we moved in with the bulldozers. You can keep them for your paper if you like, Hernandez.

'They kept pigs on a sort of communal basis,' Elliot explained. 'We used bulldozers to make a clean sweep of the place. Do you know the one thing the Chilams really objected to when we moved them down here? The concrete floors. That was the one thing that stuck in their throats. They wanted a nice earth floor so that if a kid was sick in the night or anyone couldn't be bothered to get up and go to the yard where they kept the pigs, they could make a hole and there you were.'

After that, Elliot took us to what he called the Administrative Centre. We saw a communal kitchen that was vast and

65

clean and also recently disinfected. Giant cauldrons were simmering with a mess that smelt of lime and looked like porridge. 'Posole,' Elliot said, making a face. 'You and I wouldn't eat it, but they like it. The Indians want to eat maize and beans, so maize and beans we give them. Naturally we have to pump vitamins into the stuff. Maybe in twenty years' time they'll be eating tenderized steaks and processed breakfast cereals like the rest of us. Here you see the beginning of a people's capitalism. Oh, by the way, Hernandez, here's another fact for your paper. In the one month the Project has been under way again since the liberation, our work force has averaged an increase in weight of nearly three pounds per adult.'

Something about this remark reminded me of the prison in Merida. 'Zoo animals put on weight in captivity,' I said, rather rudely. The fact was that I was beginning to be aware of a growing antipathy towards Elliot. From the beginning I had been unable to find anything much to say to him. There had been a total lack of anything in common. Now I felt a slight hostility. I put this down to his reference to planters. It was a subject on which I was very touchy.

Elliot took the small revolt mildly enough. 'Well, naturally they do. After all, most of them are getting an adequate diet for the first time. Besides that, Williams, it's not just a matter of feeding — it's psychological. The system here has been worked out with the collaboration of trained anthropologists who've made a considerable study of the Indian's make-up. Our people put on weight because in the main they're happy. Perhaps I should qualify that by saying as happy as the primitive man can be in view of his spiritual retardation and his apathy. Our mission, as I see it, is to rouse the Indian out of himself — to teach him what real happiness means, as it is to be found in creative work, in the desire to possess beautiful things, and in the will to evolve as a human being. Do you follow what I mean?'

66

The hospital followed the kitchens. 'We had to cure most of them of hookworm, malaria and syphilis before we could start treating them for anything else they happened to have picked up,' Elliot told us.

I think an undenominational church in concrete came next, then a clinic where a row of terrified-looking Indians were waiting to receive injections, and after that the crêche, staffed at the moment by buxom ladinos because the Indian women had so far shown no signs of a collective responsibility towards the rows of brown, apathetic babies who lay and gaped at the ceiling.

It was the company store that really aroused my interest. It was extraordinary. It was staffed by ladinos, too, and there was nothing to be seen but hundreds of mirrors. There were mirrors the size of large postage stamps, medium-sized mirrors, and large mirrors. Flowers and birds had been painted on the surface of some of these.

'On a tactical level our main problem's been connected with incentive research,' Elliot said cheerfully. 'We laid down a certain minimum level of efficiency that a bachelor had to reach before he could marry, that is to say, afford to rent a family chalet — I should have told you, by the way, that the bachelors are housed in separate dormitories. After that we'd played our ace card. We were hitting our heads up against the fact that these people don't ask anything from life in the way of property, so long as they have a blanket to sleep in and a couple of handfuls of maize a day ... Well now, as I see it, civilization can't start to develop until people want to possess beautiful things. So we put our best research operator to work. This character is a ladino but he speaks Chilam so well he passes off as an Indian. He told us that the only thing the Chilams showed any interest in at all was mirrors. That gave me a hunch. The Company was going into the mirror business.'

'What do you suppose they want with mirrors?' Hernandez asked.

'I guess it's something to do with magic. Some pretty darn fool idea, you can be sure. Anyway we had a special line of small mirrors made up to a cheap specification, which included silver-coating them in such a way that they couldn't be expected to last for long. What we wanted to do was to put across the idea of quality. We sold these introductory mirrors at a low figure — only ten cents, Company scrip, and the Indians certainly fell for them. There was one in nearly every chalet. After a week or two the research operator went round and pointed out that most of the mirrors were useless. I mean they wouldn't stand handling — the coating just flaked off. He told the Indians that what they ought to go in for was twenty-five cent mirrors, because these would last six months. We offered to take the old mirrors back for trade-in, and most of them fell for the idea. In the meanwhile the operator found that the Indians liked flowers and birds and that some of them who worked in the mine used to try and scratch pictures of them on the rocks. So we had the idea of introducing a line of decorated mirrors, and this went down too. Within a week we had them paying as much as one-fifty for a mirror with a couple of birds and some flowers on it. We told the store clerks to keep the best lines in the background and try to put over the idea of scarcity-value. I don't want to claim that all this amounts to more than a first step, and a pretty short step at that, but at least we can see the light ahead, and my feeling is that in five years' time things are going to look pretty different. What we are aiming at is a happy family of efficiently producing, cash-spending consumers, entitled to the same kind of rewards our civilization offers as we ourselves expect.'

I got impatient. 'I suppose this is the wrong thing to ask, but do these people have any sort of liberty? It looked to me as though you had a high wire fence round the place.'

'Doesn't it depend rather on what we mean by liberty?' Elliot asked gently.

'I never realized that the word had more than one meaning. All right then, put it this way — are they free to come and go as they please? I suppose it's conceivable that an Indian might get tired of hygienic living and mirrors, and if he does, is he allowed to walk out? Or is that an unfair question?'

'Not at all — although I'm afraid your answer is no. Not for the present. The Indians have never known liberty as we understand it. In the first place they're not a democratic people.'

'You're teaching them the meaning of true liberty, is that it?'

Elliot looked pleased, almost flattered. 'Yes. I think you might say that we are. Let's say we're doing our poor best to that end.'

'And freedom, naturally, is something quite different?'

Elliot was all patience and understanding. He laid flesh-less fingers on my arm. 'I sense a divergence in our viewpoints. Perhaps that's to be expected, and anyway I always respect the other man's opinion. That wire fence is there because a group of people have agreed to make a temporary sacrifice of their freedom in the interests, shall we say, of the true democratic liberty that you and I know and appreciate. They are undergoing an educational process, and that fence is there to protect them. Don't forget they've been at the mercy of an unprincipled band of agitators for these last five years. Then, of course, we mustn't forget the planters.'

'What mustn't we forget about them?'

'The way they treated their labour. It's always been a terrible scandal. You talk about freedom, but let me assure you that some of the tricks the planters got up to would make your hair stand on end. That was freedom for you, if you like. They thought nothing of poisoning a whole village with bootleg hooch and then having labour recruiters sign up all the men while they were drunk and drag them away. Of course they were free to come and go, only they knew darned well that if they took their freedom too seriously and cleared off home, the intendente of their village would have them beaten up and sent back rather than lose his rake-off.'

For a moment I wondered if Elliot was making a direct attack on me, but I dismissed the idea immediately. A glance at his face was enough to convince me that this was impossible. Besides, he knew nothing of my background. If anything, I would have said that Elliot rather liked me. He had given what I would have regarded as small but recognizable signs of an interest in my welfare, and of course he was the kind of man who almost fell over backwards in an effort to see two sides to a question.

We went out into Times Square again. 'Mark you,' Elliot said, 'I don't say I shouldn't have done the same thing myself if I'd been a planter. I probably would. They had plenty of worries in the days when you might as well have tried to sell seaweed as coffee. I suppose the way they figured it, the Indians had always starved.'

That was Elliot. Whenever you felt like going for him you found that he had slipped out of range. How could you pick a quarrel with a man who always saw your point of view, and who genuinely regarded you as only prevented by some easily curable blindness from seeing his?

And then again the fact had to be faced that he was right. You accepted the way Indians were treated just as you put up with brutality to animals in Mediterranean countries. For the first few months when fresh from England you felt badly about some of the things that went on, but your susceptibilities soon hardened under the influence of the example of others. There were years when the coffee crop had been completely unsaleable, and when a market could be found you were obliged to recoup your past losses as best you could. There was never any room for heartburnings over starving Indians in this order of things.

I put up with the rest of the visit without further protest. Criticism coming from me was not only pointless and ineffective, but misplaced. So I left Elliot unopposed to roll off his facts and his figures, and Hernandez to get them down in his book, and if pressed for a comment I was carefully non-committal.

I saw quite a bit of Elliot in the next few days. His slightly proprietorial attitude towards Guadaloupe rather irritated me at first, but he was quite clearly out to be helpful and friendly. He lived simply, almost austerely, with a ladino manservant to look after him, in a good-looking house about a mile outside the town. The house, built as it was from local woods, harmonized very well with its surroundings. I should have said that it had been the work of a not quite top-notch architect, but later I discovered that Elliot himself had been responsible for the design. He obviously took a good deal of pleasure in showing me over it. I was struck by the museum atmosphere of the place. There was something monastic about it too.

The living-room contained several cases of stuffed birds very ingeniously displayed in a few cubic feet of their natural environment of forest or marsh. There was a cabinet containing a vast collection of butterflies. Elliot told me that he had collected them all himself, and that he had all but seven of the different species that had been recorded in Guatemala. A wall-rack held rifles of various calibres, and there was another with an assortment of expensive-looking fishing rods. A couple of fine jaguar skins had been laid on the polished floor.

Normal furniture was sparse: three or four straight-backed chairs; a table of severe design; some book-shelves; a gramophone backed by a large polished panel covered with knobs and dials, looking like a section of a submarine's control room. There was something about this — and the other rooms as well — that was hard and angular and supremely comfortless. There was nowhere to relax in Elliot's house, and in considering this fact I found it difficult ever to imagine Elliot in a state of relaxation. I was sure too from this display of schoolboy enthusiasms, almost morbidly retained, that he had never married. When Elliot had left me for a moment I glanced at the titles of his books, expecting to gain from them some leads to the man's character. There were books about Mayan archaeology, psychology and comparative religion. Zen Buddhism and Yoga Philosophy were represented, and the *Bhagavad Gita* was there. A whole shelf was dedicated to self-improvement and the Power of Positive Thought. He did not bother with novels.

Elliot produced some good German beer, put a record on the gramophone, and twisted three or four of the knobs while lights winked and flickered on the control panel. I found we were listening to Stravinsky and the Suisse Romande. Elliot stopped twiddling the knobs and looked at me expectantly. 'What do you think of it?'

'It sounds fine to me,' I told him.

'Do you notice anything unusual about the reproduction?'

'No — I don't think so.'

'It's the latest stereophonic sound. I only installed it two days ago. You're the first person to hear it.'

'It's absolutely first class,' I said. I suppose I had come to take near-perfection for granted in these matters and I was prepared to forget about the means by which it was achieved. Nor did I really care how good the reproduction was — within limits — provided the music was there. Elliot took off the record while it was still playing. He seemed puzzled by my reaction. 'Perhaps this gives a better idea,' he said. I found myself listening to a railway engine starting off, accelerating, travelling at full speed, coming to a standstill.

'Now do you get it?' Elliot asked.

'Yes,' I said, 'I get it now.'

'It's just as if it was in this room, isn't it? I mean to say you have a complete illusion of reality.'

'I couldn't agree more.'

Elliot beamed. He lifted the pick-up arm and put it back to the start of the record, and while we sat there bolt upright on the hard chairs, drinking the good German beer, an invisible engine shunted about the room. There was no mistaking Elliot's happiness. 'I suppose that you're a lover of music too,' he said.

I nodded.

8

F OR anyone who has lived in Guatemala, other countries, by contrast, are lacking in savour. The problem confronting the people who want to promote a prosperous tourist industry is how to take out this over-strong flavour so that only the safely picturesque remains. This is difficult in a country which lies under the shadow of thirty-two volcanoes, its towns rattled constantly by earthquakes, like dice in a box, its villages peopled by a race who never smile, but sometimes giggle in a foolish way in the presence of tragedy. Tourists who visit the Indian fiestas are chilled by the fact that they are conducted in silence, and that the natives are unresponsive to kind words or gestures on the visitors' part. Worse still, if the visitors persist in staying until the evening, by which time most of the Indians are drunk, they may see machete fights when still the only sound is that of the clash of steel and the chop of a blade into a muscle and bone. The volcanoes are a scenic attraction, regular in shape and most beautiful, their ashen cones pale against the sky. It is unsafe to climb to the tops of some of them because the Indians sacrifice to their gods on altars set up on the edge of the craters, and violently resent any intrusion. The country is full of enchanters and werewolves, and its atmosphere — at least for me — is indescribably sad.

Within a few days of arriving in Guadaloupe I had begun to feel the listlessness and the depression that living in the Guatemalan highlands inevitably brought on. On Elliot's insistence I had moved into the Mayapan, and I had a suspicion that when the time came the bill might not be presented. The rooms in this hotel were all arranged so that the guests got an unimpeded view of the volcano from their window. It was one of the advertised amenities of the hotel. The Mayapan had a passion for cosy information, and one of the several notices in my room supplied all the facts the management supposed a guest would want to know. 'Through your window you will marvel at the stark majesty of the volcano Tamanzun (height 13,103 feet, name means "sighing of winds") — sacred place of the ancient Mayan gods. Tamanzun, arising from surroundings of incomparable beauty, is still held in reverence by many native tribes. One-day Pullman Pioneer Excursions arranged. All-in rate twelve dollars.'

You could soon have too much of the stark majesty of Tamanzun. Now that Hernandez had gone I was the hotel's only guest. In less than four weeks' time the Skymasters would fly in their eager cargoes and there would be plenty of activity, but now it was lifeless. Peones were still digging out the swimming pool which had to be ready, complete with subaqueous lighting, by the twelfth of the coming month. They had put up an empty showcase by the reception desk with a card which said: 'These lovely examples of traditional textiles have been woven for you personally in the Indian Village. Please inquire at desk.' An electrician from Guatemala City was fitting up an electric carillon in the jagged ruin that was all that remained of the earthquake-shattered Carmelite Convent, on the site of which the Mayapan had been built. The public rooms of the Mayapan were located in a building which followed the design of a Swiss Gasthaus, but guests were accommodated in what were called king-sized loggias, in other words cottages, spaced through the original convent gadens, which were of great charm. 'The *pito real* will sing for you in the private

75

patio of your own loggia — in which at least three varieties of orchids will usually be found in bloom.' The *pitos reales* — mocking birds — were in sumptuous gilded cages, and twice a day an Indian dressed like a Mayan noble of the New Empire would steal into the patio, fill up the birds' water container and wedge a slice of some tropical fruit in the bars of the cage; but the birds remained sullen and silent.

The flowers were all that the management claimed. There were a great many varieties, many of them possessing a repulsive beauty. They stuck out furred tongues at me from spotted throats in the depths of which small flies were digesting, and they filled the air with a sickly and funereal odour. I sat among them trying to read and became at first bored and then melancholy. I could hear the sad gourd-music tinkling in distant villages.

Guatemala is the country of the marimba, an instrument of ancient and disputed origin, consisting in its essentials of a sounding-board with a tympanum of gourds of varying sizes. You hear the marimba music everywhere. Men go to fairs, their marimbas strapped to their backs, and then stand over them all the morning, tapping out unemotional variations of four or five notes. When the first man at last tires, any bystander will take the hammers from him and go on. This was the music I heard every day, played endlessly in the street outside my window, and when, hoping to escape it, I went to a cantina, the marimba was there too. It did not seem to count for much how the marimba was played. You would see a player in the corner of the market running up and down the keys with one hand and with the other testing the quality of a shirt. The marimbas with their circles of dreaming listeners were there all the time, and in the end I could feel those patient, tireless hammers tapping not only on the keys, but at my nerve-strings.

I was becoming the prisoner of something that was almost fear, and in searching for its origins I remembered the notorious effect that Guadaloupe had always had on the planters who had come up here in the old days for a respite from the worst of the heat. After the first impact they usually announced their hope of eventually laying their bones to rest in Guadaloupe. A little later there would be complaints of loss of appetite and sleeplessness, and then of mysterious, undiagnosable sicknesses rooted in the no-man's-land between body and soul. These troubles were frequently blamed on the altitude, but some people admitted it was rather something in the atmosphere that got on their nerves. On the postage stamps they called Guatemala the Land of Eternal Springtime. But this wasn't spring. In Guadaloupe, which didn't even have a clear-cut rainy season, you were becalmed in climatic doldrums — a flaccid eternal summer among trees that bore flowers and fruit at the same time and shed autumnal leaves all the year round. Our European blood soon craved the flux of seasons denied to us by this sad paradise. There were many more Indians than ladinos in those days, and for an impressionable white man it was easy to feel the sensation of being marooned among a people, all of whom belonged to a secret society united by a silent and stealthy hatred for those whose very presence reminded them of their slavery.

Elliot, too, appeared to be a lot less cheerful as soon as Hernandez was safely off the scene. He called on me frequently, as patient and understanding as ever, but his brow slightly furrowed over the way things were going at the Project. I suspected that despite his assurances in the presence of Hernandez his Indians were being less docile than he was prepared to admit. He was very much concerned about what action I was taking in the matter of the thirteen Chilams who had gone off with the rifles, and I stalled him off as best I could. I couldn't see that thirteen Indians constituted a serious threat to the established order.

*
77

The military duties in the area were being undertaken by a patrol of ladino cavalrymen under a sergeant, and I saw no reason to interfere with these arrangements. These men were supposed to be looking for the thirteen Chilams who had gone off with the guns, and they had about as much chance of finding them as they would have had in tracking down an equal number of sand-coloured goats lost somewhere in the Sahara Desert. Every morning they rode off confidently into the forest, or up the side of a mountain, and at each village they would be met by a solemn elder carrying a gourd full of aguardiente and anxious to kiss their hands. At the second or third village, as I later learned, they were accustomed to tie up their horses and settle down to sleep off the heat of the afternoon. In the evening I used to go down to the police barracks in the main square and wait for Sergeant Calmo to ride up at the head of the returning patrol to make his report. This was unvarying and started with the noble words *Hay tranquilidad* — 'there is peace'. 'I beg leave to report there is peace, Captain. A complete absence of fresh news, with nothing stirring in the villages.' He was glassy eyed, but fine while in the saddle, although, when dismounted, he had to be held up by one of his men.

I took a great liking to these cavalrymen who were a rare and very special kind of ladino. They were all recruited from cattlemen — vaqueros they are called — who come from the cattle country down by the Pacific coast, and were members of a mysterious community who had kept to themselves and interbred for hundreds of years. They lived according to their own somewhat fierce laws, and the only personal property they permitted was a man's horse, his harness and his clothing. What was so interesting about the vaqueros was that, having taken a good look at civilization, they had consciously rejected it. Their reason, they would tell you, was that courage was the only virtue that meant anything to them, that courage came from accepting a hard, constantly active

78

life, and that the civilized way of living removed the necessity for it. A widely accepted theory was that these were the descendants of Spanish noblemen who had been exiled to this remote part of the colonies for political reasons and had married Indian women, and it was a fact that most of them had resounding old Spanish names, usually prefixed with a 'de'. When they got into trouble — it was nearly always a murder committed over a woman — they took refuge in the army, but they would not take orders from any N.C.O. who was not drawn from their own people. There were never many of them, because in the boring intervals between fighting they used to fabricate misunderstandings among themselves on fine points of honour, and kill each other in the fantastic duels that ensued.

After I had done with Sergeant Calmo and his men I usually spent an hour or two in one or other of the cantinas. A little of the flavour of the old frontier life still lingered on in these places — despite the juke-boxes — and it was difficult to keep out of quarrels with aggressive drunks. When I had had enough of parrying the deadly courtesies of men who secretly hoped they could trap me into a breach of local good manners and then shoot me with a clear conscience, I went home to bed.

The main thing, I had decided by this time, was to keep out of Elliot's way. The jungle massacre had produced in me an almost unreasoning horror of violence and bloodshed, and I wanted time to recover from what was probably nervous shock. My plan was to let sleeping dogs lie; to do everything in my power to keep out of further trouble until it was time to return to Guatemala City.

The one possible stumbling block to this campaign of masterly inactivity was, I could see, Elliot. I sensed that Elliot was the man who might stir up trouble for me; for three days I succeeded in avoiding him.

79

9

I SPENT the next three days restlessly idling. In the mornings I sat over a drink in my patio, not particularly engrossed in a book which was the only reading matter I had been able to find. This volume, which appeared to replace the Gideon Bible normally left in drawers in American hotel rooms, was entitled *The Power Within You*. It had nothing to do with mysticism but dealt with what was called the Science of Personality-Building and Self-Integration, and it made grateful acknowledgment to a number of source authors, including Mr Dale Carnegie (*How to Win Friends and Influence People*), St Paul (*The Epistle to the Corinthians*), and to none other than Mr Winthrop Elliot who was cited as author of *The Million Dollar Smile*.

This reading matter left me plenty of scope for casual observation. From where I sat I could see the top half of Tamanzun, and when a glittering speck crawled fly-like round its cone, detached itself and climbed up the sky, I recognized this for the TACA plane on the Panama-New Orleans run, and knew that it was time for lunch. In the afternoon I siesta'd. In the early evening I strolled down to the square to listen to Calmo's ritual pronouncement on the prevalence of peace. Then to the last-century, swashbuckling din of the cantina.

On the night of the third day the telephone in my room

rang for the first time. I didn't want to pick it up because I knew that Elliot would be on the other end, and that Elliot would have nothing to say that I wanted to hear.

I looked at my watch. Past ten-thirty. I had every right to be asleep. The bell went on ringing and I knew it wouldn't stop. I picked up the telephone and made my voice curt with sleep: '*Dígame*.'

'Williams — is that you? This is Elliot.'

'Yes. What's the trouble?'

'They told me you had come in. Sorry to wake you up.'

'It's all right.'

'I've some bad news. I've been trying to contact you all over the town. I heard you'd been seen in some of the bars.'

'Uh-huh.' Sleepily listening to Elliot's voice it occurred to me that it sounded better over the phone. More natural, I thought. He should always speak through a microphone.

'I'll be round there in about ten minutes.'

'Hold on,' I told him. 'I wonder if we could make it tomorrow. I'm feeling a trifle under the weather. How would eight o'clock suit you?'

I thought I noticed a new crispness come into Elliot's tone. 'I'm afraid that wouldn't do.'

'Can't we talk about it over the phone, whatever it is?'

'That's out of the question as well. No, I can't explain why. I'll tell you when I see you. Be round right away.'

I had hardly put the receiver down when the doorbell chimed in its whimsical way, reminding me that I had forgotten to disconnect it, and Elliot opened it before I could get there. He came in. 'Really I'm most terribly sorry to burst in on you like this.' He nodded at the phone. 'Never trust those things. They're liable to have the lines tapped. If it wasn't a matter of urgency, I wouldn't have bothered you. There were three deserters from the Project today.'

'I thought the government had fallen, at least,' I said. 'Can I pour you a drink?'

81

'Thanks. Whatever you're drinking will be fine.'

I went, taking my time about it, to get ice for the whisky, and I let him talk to my back. 'This is our worst setback since we got started again, and there's a particularly grave aspect to the case. It's kind of taken us by surprise.'

'It doesn't surprise me in the slightest. You won't find that wire fence of much use unless you put a watch tower in each corner and a guard with a machine-gun.'

'Are you being serious?' Elliot looked reproachful.

'No.'

'I'm afraid it's no laughing matter, you know. These were three very special cases of men who were showing some real progress.'

'Towards becoming cash-spending consumers?'

Elliot ignored this. 'We'd had them screened by the psychologist, and it was his report that made us feel justified in replacing three ladinos and putting them in charge of working parties. They were armed with rifles.'

'Didn't you tell me the whole basis of your system was voluntary?'

He was still determinedly patient. 'Our reason for issuing arms to party-leaders was that tomorrow some of the parties were on the notice-board to receive inoculations, and we figured that as they aren't quite acclimatized to the idea, this was the day they were most likely to desert if ever they felt that way. I want to say right now that no ammunition was issued. The sole purpose of the guns was to inject a little more confidence in the party-leaders.'

'Well, you certainly succeeded.' I couldn't altogether check a slight grin.

'Maybe I'm wrong about this,' Elliot said, 'and if so please forgive me, but I just can't help feeling that you, well — shall we say — aren't greatly interested? Isn't that so?'

My first impulse was to tell him that he had hit the nail right on the head, but he was beginning to look so disappointed, so much as though I'd shown myself in some way to be lacking in gratitude, that I couldn't bring myself to be so outspoken. Elliot seemed to have put on a number of years since I had last seen him. The light was frosting his thin, whitish hair, and there was a crumpled, unhappy expression about his mouth. I tried to explain my position in a reasonable manner. 'After all, you must realize that my attitude towards your labour troubles is bound to be somewhat cooler than your own. I'm here to do a certain job, and however sympathetic I personally might feel over your difficulties, they simply don't concern me officially.'

'But surely they do? Before we go any further, you realize where these men have gone, I suppose? To join the bandits.'

This irritated me. I could see my presentiments about Elliot working out accurately. I shook my head. 'But there aren't any bandits. Because people either refuse to work for you, or get tired of working for you and clear off, that doesn't automatically turn them into bandits. Not even if they do decide to take a few guns with them.'

Elliot's smile had returned instantly, and with a sense of frustration I found that he was agreeing with me. 'Why Captain, don't think I'm trying to teach you your job, or for that matter attempting to influence your opinion. I guess the only reason I've come here is to suggest a smooth and regular co-operation. Which, on the principle that two heads are better than one, might increase your effectiveness.'

'Co-operation?' I said. 'Between whom?'

'Between you and me. I use the word co-operation because I'm a firm believer in applying the democratic principle, so far as you can get it to work. I'd be very happy to feel that you and I were stringing along together without anyone being obliged to assert himself. I shouldn't enjoy having to do that at all, you know.'

I laughed. 'Really, Elliot! That's a good one. Anyone would think I was on your payroll.'

'Well, aren't you?'

I was laughing and then I felt my amusement drain away. I tried to look unconcerned. Elliot watched me closely over the top of his glass. He wasn't the kind that bluffed.

'If so, it's the first I've heard of it,' I said. This sentence sounded a lot lamer than it should have done.

'You draw two hundred a week, don't you? I hear you've just had a raise. Where do you suppose it comes from — the bright blue sky above? There wasn't a cent in the kitty when Balboa took over. Werner cleaned it right out. You knew that, didn't you?'

'I still don't quite see what all this adds up to.'

'Who do you think financed the revolution? After all, somebody had to put up the cash. It was breezed about in the press enough.'

'If you mean U.C., I thought they'd denied it.'

'Of course they denied it. How could they do anything else? You don't broadcast this kind of thing over an amplifying system. Even if we have bought up this country a couple of times, we still have to run it through a political front. If you want any further proof whose payroll you're on, I can have it sent up from the City in the form of an order from the General Staff. Believe me, I'd feel a great deal happier if that kind of action could be avoided. What I'd like to see here is a pleasant informal relationship established between us without any question of anybody handing out orders to anybody else. After all, you're going to be the partner in this outfit who has all the military experience. I may have had a little practice in the art of handling men, but I guess that's about all.'

Before I could find something to say in reply to this the earthquake started. I felt it starting up like the motors of an electric train in a distant subway, first as an isolated throb, and then I could hear it begin to move, tunnelling through the earth towards us, and after that I felt it again, this time

84

in my bones. I heard people running to open the hotel doors, and a whip of sound like cracking ice — which was the glass cracking in the window frames. My whisky splashed on the back of my hand and the light snapped out. I got up and lit the little earthquake lamp that was always kept ready. If I had been by myself I should have gone out into the patio as a matter of normal prudence, but Elliot hadn't moved and I knew he wouldn't. The heavy electric-light fitting was swinging over his head and he had just asked me some question, but I had lost my train of thought and could not concentrate on what he was saying. He gave not the slightest sign of having noticed what was happening. I was not sure that there wasn't a trace of gentle amusement in his expression as he watched me. The shock was dying down in an uneasy distant rumble.

'Two hundred a week is as much as a general pulls down in most armies. In my view that's a generous sum. In my view also you're the kind of man who would want to feel he was fulfilling his side of the contract — and when I say fulfilling it, I naturally mean with a good will.'

I could hear them still running about in the street, probably carrying out into the open all they could grab. They have as many as fifty earthquakes a year in Guadaloupe. Sometimes a second shock follows the first, and it is always worse, and if there is a third shock it is worse still. I resented Elliot's humiliating calm. 'I shall certainly fulfil my obligations,' I told him. 'I think it's the efficiency rather than the goodwill that counts,' I added coldly.

'All right. We'll forget the good will then and concentrate on the efficiency.' Elliot was resolutely pleasant.

'You may rest assured that I shall take whatever measures I think necessary to deal with any situation that may arise.' This was meant to be a dignified brush-off, but when I said it it sounded feeble.

'Fine,' Elliot said. 'So long as they get taken, and get taken fast, because this place is going to open as a tourist resort in three weeks' time and it's going to have to be as safe as White Sulphur Springs by that date. What are your plans, Captain?'

'At the moment, I'd prefer not to discuss them, but I gather you'd feel quite happy if your deserters gave themselves up and turned in the guns.'

'Yes, I guess I would.'

'Then may we leave it at that?'

'Very well. So be it; but I certainly hope you'll remember that this situation is a potentially explosive one, and unless some kind of effective action is taken right now the Company may find itself with a full-scale mutiny on its hands.'

I saw no point in prolonging the topic, so I didn't say anything in reply to this. I was just going to say 'Well, I think if you don't mind I'll turn in now,' when Elliot said: 'Oh yes, there was one other thing. Do you remember I mentioned we were fixing up regular excursions to the crater of Tamanzun?'

'The Pioneer Pullmans — or is it the Pullman Pioneers?'

'Whichever way you like.' Elliot's tone had become indulgent. 'We had the old mule trail fixed up so that you can get up there in a jeep, and I want to say this right now, you don't appreciate what a panorama can really be like until you've done this trip. Don't forget to take a camera along when you go or you'll want to kick yourself.'

'I'm not terribly interested in photography.'

'Well, that's a pity. Anyway you'll enjoy the trip. As I was saying, we're taking the visitors up in jeeps, and the Indians up there have had notice to quit. You'd never stop the tourists from taking photographs of them, and the first time anyone got his camera out the Indians would throw rocks at him. That's what happened the last time a party made the trip. We had a proper Court injunction served to restrain them from denying freedom of access to a natural

86

beauty spot. We're giving them a day or two to clear away their junk, and then the police are going up to make sure they've pulled out, and if they haven't they're going to take them inside. I'd appreciate it if your men went along.'

'It's not exactly a part of their duties, is it?'

'No, of course it's not. This is strictly a matter for the police, and the police are going to do whatever has to be done. But the way I figure it is that you and I are out to avoid all the trouble we can, and if a few soldiers showed up there with the police there wouldn't be any chance of an argument getting started.'

'I'd like to think about it before committing myself,' I said. 'Perhaps I could have a glance at that Court order.'

'Why certainly. Miguel the intendente has it. I'll have him bring it over tomorrow.' Elliot drained his glass and put it down with finality. 'Well, I still have a few things to attend to, so I'll be getting along. Doesn't look like we're in for any more excitement tonight. Every time we get a shake I always wonder just how much more that old church tower can take.' He held out his hand. 'Good night, Williams. I'll have Miguel bring that order round in the morning.'

I went out into the street with him. The people were still walking up and down carrying lamps, afraid to go into their houses. It was a dark night, and Tamanzun showed as a black triangle on the stars. There were pin-points of red fire at its apex, where the Indian shamans were tending their sacrificial altars, and I was quite sure that in a few days those fires would be extinguished for ever.

After Elliot had gone I couldn't settle down, so I groped my way down to the plaza. It had been raining, and before I got to the end of the Calle Barrios the lamps came on again, filling the pools in the flagstones with reflections of charging bulls and blood, of blue dye and the dreamy poster-faces of cigarette smokers. It was quiet in between the juke-box music; so quiet that you could hear the distant, frustrated yappings of coyotes under the hen-houses in the trees. I walked about the streets for at least a couple of hours, trying to calm my thoughts, and then, when I thought there might be some chance of sleeping, I went back to bed.

———

10

THE next day produced the surprise of my life. Greta suddenly appeared. I wandered into the bar of the Mayapan for my morning reviver — it had been empty ever since Hernandez left — and Greta was there. She let out a little shriek and held out her arms and we hugged each other. That was how it had always happened — this generous welcome that swept away my premeditated reserves. And this time I had had no warning that would have given me time to prepare my defences. 'Darling, they told me you were here, and I simply had to break my journey. I'm on my way to Coban.'

I squeezed her again. 'Coban?' I said.

'Yes, I'm going home; but the next plane goes on Thursday, so we can have two lovely days together. That's if you want to.'

Two days, I thought. I was like a reformed alcoholic suddenly faced with unforeseen temptation and looking for an excuse for indulgence. What danger could there be in two days? Knowing my infirmities I was ready to agree that a week might prove fatal. But two days . . . I looked at her cautiously, at the same time noting in myself the familiar breathlessness and excitement as of old. Looking down at her face I saw for the first time, drawn in the skin just below the corners of the eyes, the little dry creases which one day would deepen into wrinkles. She's ageing quickly, I thought, and then smiled to myself at the way I was throwing up my barricades. This was the way it had always been; the quick moment of revelation that came with every reunion, but that faded so rapidly, to be followed by a renewed illusion.

We sat down again and I ordered drinks. I talked to her and held her hands. 'Happy?' I asked.

'No. I'm very unhappy. That's the reason I'm going home.'

'But Coban — why Coban?' I asked. And then I remembered. I had always thought of Greta as a product of Guatemala City. But, of course, she had been born in Coban, and she was a notable example of the great speciality of that area — beautiful women produced by the union of the German planters with the pick of the local Indian women.

'I saw Don Arturo in Guatemala City the other day,' I told her. 'I gathered from something he said that things hadn't been too well with you.'

'Don't let's speak about it,' she said, squeezing my hands. 'I want to forget that Guatemala City ever existed.'

'All right, we won't speak about it.' I had a pretty good idea of the nature of the troubles that happened to Greta, and I was quite content to leave them undefined. Greta was originally the victim of Freud — of Freud transformed by the misrepresentation of the popular digests, so that the pioneer of new ways to mental health finally appeared in Central America as a prophet of self-destruction. The only crime in Greta's post-war set had been self-restraint — inhibition it was called, and Greta had certainly freed herself from any possibility of imputation of this heresy.

'You're here now, that's the important thing.' It was a strange fact that when I was with Greta it was hard to associate her with what went on when we were not together. All that was necessary was a trick of forgetting, which I sometimes managed to perform, for us to be completely happy. 'What on earth are you going to Coban for?' I asked.

'I don't know. I just want to get away from things and go back home. I'll probably end by marrying an Indian.'

'Rubbish.' I laughed.

'It's not rubbish at all. I mean it.' I noticed that her eyes were watering.

'I can imagine you in a mud hut, slapping up tortillas, with a kid tied on your back.' The last part of this remark came out before I could stop myself and then, for the first time for years, I felt myself flush. Greta had sacrificed her ability to have children on the altar of the god of freedom from inhibition. I turned my face away quickly, but I was sure that she had seen my change of colour.

Now she was defiant. 'I lived in a mud hut until I was twelve. They were the best times I ever had. I never saw a white man until my father came back from Germany and sent me to school in Guatemala City.'

'This,' I said, 'I have heard before. And more than once. In a moment you're going to tell me that you feel more Indian than German.'

'Yes I do. Of course I do.'

'Of course you don't, and the very fact that you say things like that proves it. You're the purest kind of German romantic. The Germans invented that kind of attitude. First of all you go and change your name to Greta when you thought it was romantic to be German. Now, I suppose you'll change it back again. How can I take you seriously?'

'David,' she said. 'Something's happened to you since I saw you last. You're changing. Where's your sense of humour gone? Buy me another nice drink and let's change the subject.' She had herself under control again.

'They turned you into a German at the German school. I've never seen such a transformation in anyone. We all agree that you're less happy than you would have been in the mud hut in your mother's village, but — well, let's be realistic — it's a bit late to do anything about it now.'

'Please!' she said. 'Do let's talk about you for a change. What are you supposed to be doing here? They told me you'd finished up as a South American General.'

I outlined the situation for her, and then she wanted to make plans for her two days' stay. She soon brightened up. 'Darling, we're going to have a simply wonderful time together. I want to see all those wonderful things they tell you about in the prospectus — the volcano, and the haunted lake and the jaguars. Have you heard a jaguar yet?'

'You mean "the blood-chilling cough of the big cat heard at sundown as you take your ease in the patio of your loggia under the tropic sky". No, I haven't. Nor has anyone else. They're miles away down in the jungle, and in any case they don't make that kind of noise.' I thought for a moment. 'We'd better rule out the volcano because the Indians up there have just been told to clear out and they may not be feeling very well-disposed towards whites. That leaves the lake. You'll like that. I think we ought to make the trip before Elliot puts it off-limits to military personnel. Let's go as soon as we can.'

She was enthusiastic at once. 'Why not today? Let's go today. Are there any fish? I want to fish. We'll catch a lot of mojarras. And after we've had our picnic, we'll have a lovely swim. Oh David, it's going to be wonderful!'

We went up to the lake in one of Elliot's jeeps. The outstanding thing about Lake Tenyuchin, which possibly has something to do with its height above sea level, is that seen from above, as the road winds down to it, it is a deep and unnatural purple, although the water, when you are on the lake in a boat, is black. We bought some crabs for bait and borrowed a cayuco from the lake Indians and fished for mojarras. The mojarras were easy to catch, but they were small. There was nothing but mojarras and crabs in this lake. About every five minutes Greta would pull up her line with a three-inch fish on the hook. She had had a lot of experience at mojarra fishing as a child and was very expert. Her enthusiasm was as inexhaustible as it was easy to stimulate. Every time she brought a fish into the boat she gave a little scream of delight. She wanted to go on fishing all day, but after we had about twenty fish between us I persuaded her to give up. Then we paddled over to see the rock where, when the Spanish were approaching, one of the Indian tribes had committed suicide en masse at the order of their chiefs by throwing themselves into the lake. This was the origin of the story of the lake's being haunted.

It was one of those brilliant, hard, Guatemalan days when even the clouds seem as solid and permanent in the landscape as the mountains themselves, and their marbled reflections were piled up in the middle of the lake. It was hot. The sun sparkled on the black surface of the water as we cut into it with our paddles. Greta's blouse of acid green, specially put on for the excursion, was the only jarring note in the fierce harmonies that surrounded us.

After we had visited the suicide rock we went on to the far shore, lit a fire, stuck little skewers of cane through the fish, and grilled them. Then Greta wanted to swim. She took off all her clothes and went down to the water. She would not have had the slightest hesitation in doing this in front of any man, and had anyone seemed surprised she would have argued that it showed the innocence of her mind and that her early background made it very easy for her to go back to nature in ways like this. But I knew that it was a thing that no Indian girl would ever have done, and that it was more of an act of homage to magazine-feature Freud than it was native innocence.

There was a fishing village at the back of the shingle beach, half hidden by the cane. It was a place that had had some importance, but the earthquakes had smashed it up, and the cupola of the church had fallen to one side and was

93

cracked all round like an egg. I was not sure what the Indians might think about our going back to nature outside their village, so I kept my shorts on. Greta went into the water naked. I tried not to look at her too much, because although at the moment I was safe, I did not know how much temptation I could stand. Greta, who dressed without taste, came into her own when she took off her clothes. She had her father's blond hair and her mother's dark skin and neat Indian body. The revelation of golden down at the meeting of her brown thighs would have disturbed the thoughts of an anchorite. The physical signs were the only thing Indian about her. Education is all that really counts.

We swam out a good way. The water was cold, and although it was black it was transparent and I could see the details of Greta's firm, brown body beneath the surface. I did not enjoy this swim because I was thinking about having to go back to the village with the fisher-folk watching us through their fences. When we reached the beach it was worse than I had expected. A line of men and women were waiting for us. They were puny and wretched-looking and two of the women had huge goitres. I took an immediate dislike to them. Very miserable people are apt to look vicious, and we naturally forget about their misery and blame them for this seeming depravity.

I waved to them from the water to go away and they retreated sullenly, but one of the men shouted something in an angry voice. We sat down on the shingle and shivered in the sun. We could hear people moving about out of sight behind their fences and some small, ugly dogs came out and rushed at us, barking and then backing away. I was half turned from Greta but I could see her out of the corner of my eye putting on her skirt and blouse. 'They are very angry with us,' she said in a hurt voice. 'They don't like white people to come to this village.'

'How do you know?'

'I understood what the man said. He said we are driving all the fish away. They think that all animals are just as much afraid of the whites as they are.'

We finished dressing and went down to the water's edge. I tried to feel unconcerned, but the Indians had come out from behind their fences again, and I could hear them following us. Their dogs were snarling and snapping at our heels. When we stopped and turned round suddenly, the Indians stopped too and stood there watching us with a kind of furtive hatred. We pushed the cayuco clear of the shingle, clambered in and paddled away from the shore. Stones began to splash in the water all round, and a single pebble fell in the boat. Some of the men even waded after us, shouting and waving their hands.

I felt depressed about this incident. At that moment I think I really hated Indians. All Indians. 'I must recommend Elliot to include this spot in one of his luxury Pioneer itineraries,' I said bitterly.

'They feel so terribly weak,' Greta said. 'The whites are ogres for them. Some of the Indians think that we live for ever.'

'And when this kind of thing happens you realize how far apart from them you really are.'

'Yes,' she said, 'I suppose I do.'

She didn't appear to want to talk either, and we paddled down to the end of the lake in silence. It was late afternoon now and the frosty brilliance had gone out of the air, and when we landed the eagles were fishing close inshore. You could not see the eagle's dive against the curtain of the mountain in shadow, but only the white upward spurt of water as it struck. We found the jeep and drove quickly down to Guadaloupe. I had a guilty feeling growing in me, like a boy who has been playing truant, and with it a presentiment that something had happened while I had been away. As indeed it had.

―――――――

11

I FOUND Miguel the intendente waiting for me in the smok-
ing-room of the Mayapan. Greta went to her room. I
told her that I'd come and collect her within the hour, and
then I went back to deal with Miguel. A boy in Elliot's
fancy-dress uniform, who had been lurking in the background watching him unhappily, bowed himself out as I
came in, and Miguel screwed round his big head to look
after him, and spat into the polished bowl of a spittoon.

He sat, an uneasy pyramid of flesh, formally black-clad, in
a deep chair, and didn't get up. He exuded a confident and
surly familiarity, and when he nodded to the chair opposite
him, and I sat down, his breath, spirit-laden, surged towards
me across two intervening yards of delicately 'sanitized'
Mayapan air. His silver-mounted staff of office lay across
the table.

'Well,' he said, 'they've turned up as foreseen — sixteen of
them. They cleared a ladino village out of food only five
miles away, and I don't mind telling you this the shop-
keepers in this town have lost their grip on their bowels.'

The extremely unpleasant effect upon me of this information was perhaps lessened by my surprise at the way in which
Miguel imparted it. There is no language like Spanish for
expressing the extremes of punctilio or ribald familiarity. I'd
never heard of an Indian addressing a white like this before.
He usually sounds like an N.C.O. speaking to an officer
and carefully chooses long and elaborate words such as the

equivalent of 'proceed' instead of go, and 'undertake' instead of do. This coarse and democratic brevity came as a shock, but I decided to overlook it so long as the man said what he felt like saying. From the beginning I'd suspected him of being capable of honesty. I pushed a packet of cigarettes at him and he waved them away — another extraordinary breach of manners by local standards. 'And now what's to be done?' I asked.

'What's to be done?' He bared his brown teeth in what was supposed to be a laugh. 'Why — finish them off, of course. Now they've eaten. As soon as their bellies are empty they'll rob again.'

'I asked you to do your best to contact them. Were you able to do so?'

'No. I didn't try. They're a lot of *cabrones* but they're not fools.' The word *cabrón* is really untranslatable. It means something between idiot and swine. There is not much anger in it, but it is loaded with contempt.

'You've fallen down on your job,' I told him.

He managed to look surprised. At first he seemed expressionless, but later it was possible to recognize the small betraying squirm of muscles under the brown leather of his face, the sharp refocusing of a speculative black eye. Slyness and malice were there, suspicion and probably contempt, too, but above all suspicion.

'You want to talk to them? You're wasting your time. Look here, I'll tell you what to do. You do your part and I'll do mine.' He stopped. 'Half a minute. I want a drink. Here, you!' he called to the boy cringing in a far doorway, 'bring me a bottle of whisky.' Whisky, I thought, how on earth can he afford whisky? And then the answer came to me. I remembered something that Elliot had let drop in explanation of the strange fact that an Indian should hold an office the equivalent of mayor. He was the last of the Chilam nobility, Elliot had mentioned, and therefore a useful man to have about, and — Elliot had gone on to hint — all the more useful as the result of an expensive taste in liquor. 'But for all that,' he had added, 'the guy doesn't like me. Don't ask me why. I've certainly done my darnedest to understand what makes him tick.'

'The government has aeroplanes, hasn't it?' He was watching me closely. 'Well then, there you are. That's your answer. You don't have to risk your skin.'

'And you think I'm afraid to risk my skin?'

'You want to talk. It's the same thing. When you have enemies you kill them. If you want to talk things over, it means you're not strong enough to do anything else.' He called me 'tu' all the time. It wasn't so long ago since I would have had him thrown out. Have I made some progress, I wondered, or is it really nothing more than a failing nerve?

Miguel shifted and scratched. His cheeks and forehead were covered with tiny drops of sweat. He must have been sweltering in the thick, black suit. 'Tell them to send an aeroplane and I will do my part.'

'Are you a Chilam?' I asked him.

'Yes. I am a Chilam.'

I shook my head. I couldn't understand the man.

'The Chilams are cabrones. If the plane comes now there will be only sixteen to kill. Next week it will be fifty. The week after that perhaps all the Chilams. However many there are to kill, it is easy for the planes. We saw how the planes killed them in the revolution.'

The whisky came on a tray with two glasses. Miguel picked up the bottle and inspected it closely. Ben Nevis said the label, and beneath this title a kilted Highlander waved his broadsword at us, but there was something tropical about the glen in the background, and in this picture the famous peak somehow resembled a volcano. The intendente drove the boy away and skewered the cork out with his knife. He

98

poured out two half-tumblers of the whisky, and gulped down his own. The boy was backing away. 'Come here, you,' he said. 'Now, look at that cabrón. He's more of a cabrón than a ladino is. What's your name, cabrón?'

'Antonio Cluj.' The boy was looking down at his feet. He was one of Elliot's star pupils, with a sensational I.Q.

'No it isn't — it's cabrón. Understand that? Cabrón. Aren't you going to kiss my hand? Where did you get those clothes, cabrón? Your father was Antonio Cluj, but your mother had you by one of those half-whites that go round the villages selling chancre ointment.'

Listening to this outpouring of scorn I was beginning to form a new theory. Miguel didn't like Elliot, and it looked as though he detested anyone like this boy who had come under Elliot's influence. His irreverent handling of the Mayapan's furniture, the disdainful glances he threw about him and his rudeness to me, all combined to suggest that he hated the whites and all they stood for — above all, I should have imagined, the Chilam Project. This caused me to wonder if, after all, this talk of planes and bombing — the apparent callousness over the fate of his own people — might not be a pretence. Could it be that Miguel was sounding me all the time, making certain that I was completely genuine, in the matter of assurances I had already given him before he decided to co-operate?

'You know where these men are, don't you?' I threw the question at him suddenly.

He was sipping his second whisky, and for a moment my question stopped him. The black pupils of his eyes suddenly appeared over the rim of the glass. Then they dropped out of sight. He went on swallowing till the glass was empty, put it down and wiped his mouth with the back of his hand. 'No, I don't know,' he said.

'But you could find out?'

'I am a government official. No Indian ever comes to my

99

office. No one gives information to government officials.'

'You are also the head of a tribe, and nothing in that tribe is ever done without your knowledge.'

No reaction. Whether or not Miguel was the head of the tribe I didn't know, nor did I believe it was a thing known by any white. The Indians never answered questions of this kind.

'The planes?' Miguel said, completely ignoring my previous remark. 'Would the government send planes?'

'No,' I told him, 'on no account.' What a tremendous effect upon them the sight of planes in action had had, I thought. Miguel must have seen the Thunderbolts doing their work.

He shrugged his shoulders and got up. 'In that case then ...' The whisky bottle took his eye, and he poured out another half tumblerful of spirit, and threw some money on the tray. I counted it. Five quetzals — a fortune for an Indian to spend on drink. 'Bring the change, cabron,' he said to the boy. He looked after him, shaking his head. Then he spat in the spittoon. 'All true Chilams are born with a blue spot on their backsides. There won't be many more of them.' He got up. 'Before I go, you had better see this.' He pulled out a piece of dirty, creased paper with a seal on it, and handed it to me. I read it. It was the warrant for the removal of the shamans' altars from the crater of Tamanzun.

'It seems to be all in order.' I handed it back to him.

'We're going to execute it on Monday.'

'Do you expect any resistance?'

'Would you expect any resistance from half a dozen old men all doubled up with rheumatism? It's cold up there at nights. It gets into the bones.'

'I'll be expecting to receive the other information from you,' I told him.

He picked up the bottle of whisky, stared at it and put it down again. Then he turned round and walked off quickly on his short legs. It was surprising to see that a man with such a big, heavy body should be so short when he stood up, and it was also surprising that he could move so quickly. As he went through the door he struck the head off a lily with the silver-topped staff of office. A boy watering the flowers in the garden saw him coming and shot away down a side path. These people could be very hard on their own kind.

12

THAT evening Greta and I did a round of the cantinas. For many people they are a part of the attraction of Guadaloupe, and they have about them a certain poetry of the kind that sometimes associates itself with seediness and poverty and vice. The owners of the cantinas give them sentimental names and daub their walls with savage colours. They spread fresh pine-needles on the floor, just as sawdust is used in other parts of the world. The scent from the pine-needles, mixed with the fierce, etheric odours of spilt liquor, gives the cantinas a very special and distinctive aroma. Half-starved-looking ne'er-do-wells make up the majority of the customers. They live on corn-leaf cigarettes, cheap spirits and the passionate Latin-American music dispensed by the juke-boxes.

We went first to 'My Bet', which I remembered in the old days as being called 'I Seek My Beloved'. This dive had been renamed as the result of a recent and celebrated wager when one customer had bet another that he would not shoot the first man to come through the door. The verdict was manslaughter, not murder.

It was still considered not a good thing to spend too much time in 'My Bet', but Greta insisted on going there. Afterwards we took in 'The Noble Visitor', and 'I Await Thee on Thy Return', and finally we settled down in 'Thou and I'. You could relax in comparative safety in 'Thou and I', which exploited the romantic aspect of Guadaloupe's night life. It had been accidentally burnt down and then carefully rebuilt in the style of a Dodge City saloon of about 1875, as observed on the movies. It possessed a resident guitarist, who had been reprieved many years before after beheading a faithless mistress. There was a staff of girls with clouds of lovely, dark hair, and tragic faces. Having drunk a glass of aguardiente in each of the preceding cantinas, we were both very happy by the time we reached 'Thou and I', and I was becoming a little reckless. An idea had suggested itself of trying to persuade Greta not to go on to Coban but to stay with me. It was not an idea that I could surrender to immediately, even in my present elevated state. In fact the warm alcoholic haze in which I was floating was still shot through with flashes of caution and sanity. I could still see (but all the time less distinctly) that no good could come of a surrender to this impulse. My safety lay in the two-day time limit that Greta herself had imposed.

The guitarist, who was small, gentle-looking and middle-aged, now came and sang, with great feeling, of love betrayed — the favourite theme of Central-American minstrelsy. This, unfortunately, after an excess of aguardiente was bound to wake in me a responsive ache.

I had lived with Greta for three brief periods before finally leaving Guatemala, and I had even considered marrying her. Over two years had passed since the last episode had come to an end.

Greta, when she lived with me, blithely betrayed me with many others, and when she went off to live with other men, she of course betrayed them with me. What I complained of most was that she did this behind a façade of innocence in which it was very easy to believe. When cornered, so that further deceits were hopeless, she claimed exemption from normal standards on some remote grounds connected with her ancestry. I must have carried with me the special

odour of cuckoldry, discernible — it is believed in Guatemala — even by dogs. More than once in those quarters
of Latin-American cities — usually in the vicinity of railway stations — where street photographers, pedlars of cheap
crockery, and cartomancers gather, a fortune-teller had
muttered at my back the warning formula: *no es el engaño sino
la duda que mata* — 'it is not the betrayal but the doubt that
kills'. The Spanish word *perfidiosa* described Greta well —
although it is less severe than its English equivalent and can
even be reproachfully affectionate in its application. She
was, however, beautiful, generous, tolerant and compas-
sionate — a compendium of many virtues, in fact, except
the important and self-preserving one of honesty. Through
the lack of this and its physical consequences she had fallen
a victim to crones who, with their probings, had finally deprived her of her hope of motherhood. In the attempt to
account for Greta's fatal weakness, I reached the conclusion
that a purely physical diagnosis would not meet the case.
What she suffered from was an almost unhealthy craving to
be loved all the time. It was not merely sexual intercourse
she wanted. She couldn't tolerate the benevolent decline
into which even the most fevered of loves must eventually
settle, and at the first sign of this she would quietly look
elsewhere. So far as I could see she was without discrimina-
tion. Very affectionate people usually are.

Aguardiente is a great stimulant to this kind of brooding,
and the forlorn ballads of the guitarist continued to do their
work. I was saved by a member of the company who, having
had enough of betrayals, put a coin into the juke-box, which
began to rattle out a *paso doble*, regularly used as a rather
boisterous antidote to too much musical heart-burning.

Greta, who rarely suffered from nostalgia, wanted to
dance, and after that I felt better. I came out of myself.
Beginning to pay attention to the surroundings, I noticed at
once that there were far more bar-flies than usual. The

cantina was full of new ladino faces, and these newcomers were even tougher-looking than the habitués, and some of them — despite an emergency order prohibiting the carrying of firearms — obviously had guns in their pockets. There was clearly nothing that I could do about this very disturbing fact, but I could see that action would have to be taken quickly. If all the bars were like this, the town must be full of desperadoes.

The ladinos were very polite. They smiled slightly and bowed if they caught us looking in their direction, and presently one came over to our table, removed his hat with a flourish worthy of an eighteenth-century nobleman, and asked me if I would care to see some cheap jewellery. The cantinas provide a sort of indoor market for articles of this kind, and although many buyers prefer to believe that they are buying stolen goods, most of them are offered for sale by people who are temporarily short of money. However, there are conventions to be observed. The seller is supposed to attract one's attention in a surreptitious way, and it is a courtesy on the potential buyer's part to enter into the spirit of the thing and hush his tone accordingly.

After bowing for the second time, our friend asked permission to sit down. He untied a handkerchief, scooped up the contents and passed them to me under the table. I showed them to Greta, doing my best to keep up the part. There were several rings and loose stones. 'Good fakes, aren't they?' I said to Greta in English.

I suddenly felt a happy recklessness — a reaction, probably from my recent mood — and I wanted to do something to fix this evening, and this moment, in my memory. I wanted to buy Greta a ring. A genuine ring. Not something with a huge, worthless stone. The difficulty was how to explain to the ladino what I wanted without conveying the offensive implication that what he had already offered me was false. 'Something perhaps a little smaller,' I said. 'Very good —

you realize — but not quite so large. Please understand me, I don't speak for myself, but some people are always ready to assume a large stone cannot be genuine.'

The ladino understood. Smiling secretly, he produced another ring from the pocket of his shirt. He twisted it slowly, and the diamond concentrated all the light in the room and shot it at me in a yellow flame. 'Two hundred,' he whispered to me. I knew that he had named his lowest price, because with a lady present there was no possibility of haggling for either of us. 'It's worth five times the price,' the ladino whispered. It probably was, and I wondered whether he might be selling it on commission for one of the rich shop-keepers, who, as Miguel had suggested, were feeling panicky, and therefore anxious to get their hands on cash. I gave him ten twenty-quetzal notes, and he smiled again and, bowing, backed away as if from the presence of royalty.

This could have been one of the turning points of my life, because I was certain that Greta had changed. She was different in some important way. I could not place my finger on the nature of this change, but I suspected that at last something had happened to open her eyes to a realiza-tion of the fate she was heading for. I was going to ask her to stay with me and to give up the idea of going to Coban. She was in raptures over the ring, and I took her hand and began to put it on a finger. She was looking at me wide-eyed and then down at the ring, and suddenly it came to me through my half-drunken haze and confusion that I was making a mistake. The ring was on her engagement finger. It was an unforgivable blunder, and I made it worse by try-ing to laugh it off as I removed the ring again and put it on the second finger of the right hand. She may even have thought that this was some kind of stupid, premeditated joke. Her expression changed and there was a long and terrible silence. She took the ring off, looked at it and re-placed it. I was afraid she was going to give it back to me.

The evening had collapsed and I found that I had become quite sober and could think of nothing to say.

Shortly afterwards we went back to the hotel. I thought it good policy to leave Greta at the door of her room, consoling myself with the thought that I still had a clear twenty-four hours in which to put things right. Ten minutes later when I changed my mind and went back and tapped on the door, there was no reply.

———

13

I GOT up early next morning and when I was having breakfast the smooth ladino reception clerk came to my table
with an envelope. He professed to have no knowledge to
where it had come from. It had not been handed in when he
had been on duty. I slit open the envelope and took out a
sheet of the wretched quality squared paper they used locally. The word Julapa was written across it in big broken-
up capitals. The word rang a bell. I folded up the paper
and put it away. 'Julapa,' I said to the clerk before I could
check myself. 'Where's Julapa?' It was a mistake to have
asked him. He pointed it out on a map lately painted on one
of the walls. On this map half the country was blotted out
by orchids, jaguars and tapirs, but Julapa had been left uncovered. It was a village down in the hot country, twenty
miles away. 'Here be divers forest dwellers' was written in
some sort of semi-gothic characters by the red circle indicat-
ing the village.

I could not have been more happy that I had happened to
pick this up when I did — I assumed it to have come from
Miguel — because hardly ten minutes later Elliot appeared
on the scene. I heard his jeep slide up to the door, and the
soft gulp and wail coming from the golden throat of his
radio, and then his quick footfall, light almost as a child's,
as he ran up the steps. He was whistling softly. I caught myself straightening up, trying to look as though I had some
special purpose in being where I was, and then Elliot was

through the door, hand outstretched and looking surprised and pleased to see me.

'Hullo there. I didn't see you about yesterday, so I thought I'd stop by and say *que tal?* He was cool and crisp in his tight starched collar and small bow. Elliot never seemed to notice the weather. We exchanged hand grips and I felt the small finger-bones crack slightly.

'I was up at the lake most of the day, having a look round,' I told him.

'Yes, I heard you were. Grand up there, isn't it? We're thinking of organizing a dude ranch with aquatic sports facilities. Maybe next year . . . Say, how about going into the writing-room? It's liable to be cooler there in the morning.'

We went into the writing-room, where the new picture of the President now hung. He looked a lot fiercer now than I remembered him as being. 'Long Live Balboa the Liberator', it said underneath. There was nothing about justice this time. Elliot looked up and seemed to see the picture for the first time too. 'For Pete's sake!' he said, 'that quite had me startled for a moment. I thought it was Werner back again.'

We both laughed.

'Pick up anything new at the lake?' Elliot asked. I was sure he knew how I had spent the day, but there was no malice in the remark.

'Nothing very much, to tell the truth. But the main thing, I think, is to keep on the move and — well — absorb the feeling. Keep one's ear to the ground.' I was surprised to find that I was trying to justify myself to Elliot.

'That's the idea all right. I hope you took one of the jeeps.'

'I did. I thought it would be all right.'

'Of course. At any time. You know you don't have to ask me. See anything of the lake Indians?'

'There were a few of them about. Rather a miserable looking collection.'

'They're not a box-office attraction, are they? To be frank, I'm all out to rope them into the Project as soon as we can find room for them. You know, I begin to understand how missionaries must feel about making converts when I see how these people drag their arses through life. The problem is how to get it into their heads that we're out to save them from extinction — because that's what it amounts to. We had five more deserters this morning. Only discovered it at roll call. Sometimes I feel a little disheartened.'

'Armed trusties again?' I opened my mouth to ask, but I stopped myself.

'Five very promising chaps from the bachelors' dormitory,' Elliot said. 'They broke out and went over the fence during the night, which means we're going to have to electrify the wire. I'm sorry about that. We sent out search parties right away, but once they reach the jungle it's hopeless.'

'So that makes twenty-one now. Always assuming that they've joined forces with the others.'

'I guess that's the assumption we have to work on. For my money it's a pretty safe bet. What has me really worried is that there's quite a panic starting up in the town. By that I don't mean they're running about tearing out their hair by handfuls, but they've certainly got the idea that things aren't looking too bright. The morning train was full of people pulling out in a hurry. There's a lot of loot to be had in this town, and these people don't forget what happened last time there was an Indian revolt. You could have washed your feet in the blood running down the gutters, so they say. I gave Miguel a couple of bottles of Scotch, and told him to see that the shops kept open. By the way, David, how are your investigations coming along?'

'As it happens,' I told him, 'not too badly. In fact, not badly at all. It was rather slow going at first. It had to be while we were getting the lie of the land, but things are beginning to move at last.'

'That's very gratifying news. You mean you're actually on to something definite?'

'I believe so. That is to say, as far as one can be sure of anything in this life.'

'Well, that's great. I don't mind confessing — no offence, of course — that it comes as kind of a pleasant surprise too. Believe me, I appreciate what you've been up against. The way I saw it you were boxing some pretty heavy odds. Any hope of some conclusive action soon?'

'It's a bit difficult to make promises at this stage, but — well — I don't see why not. Give me another couple of days and I ought to have some news for you.'

'Well, that's fine. That's really something. Am I to understand, by the way, that you've actually located the hideout?'

I hesitated. 'Well, I don't know about that at this stage. There's a good chance of it. Put it this way, I've had some information from what I believe to be a reliable source.'

A wistful expression had come into Elliot's face, like a child with his nose pressed to a shop-window full of expensive toys.

'When are you planning to move in on them?'

'I'm not sure. The first thing is to make a reconnaissance trip.' I thought quickly. I wanted to forestall any offer of help. 'I'm going by myself.'

Elliot looked disappointed. 'Isn't that taking a bit of a risk?'

'It's a risk that has to be taken. If I went with an escort it would mean one of two things. They'd hear that we were coming and clear off, or there would be a battle which, naturally, I'm going to avoid if I can.'

'How about fixing up a little surprise?' Elliot asked. 'As a matter of fact I wish you would give some consideration to the possibility of our joining forces. We have the municipal guards and the company police to draw on. What's wrong with surrounding the place — whatever it is — at night?'

'There'd still be a battle.'

'But the odds would be two or three to one. Plus the element of surprise.' Elliot's expression became thoughtful. 'Another great help would be a couple of machine-guns — last-but-one pattern U.S. Army Brownings we shipped in last week.'

'I'm afraid I'm obliged to give them every chance to surrender first. In the first place because those are the terms I've offered, and secondly because I had personal instructions from the President himself on this point, and they were to use conciliatory measures.'

'The President!' Elliot laughed gently. By a common impulse we both glanced up at the new portrait and the President scowled back at us. 'Between you and me and these four walls I would be inclined to say that the President knows as much about conciliation as a mountain lion who hasn't eaten for a week. Anyway, that's beside the point. What were the terms you offered?'

'They were simple enough. They hand over the guns and they get a free pardon. To be realistic, you must admit that nothing less would produce any result. Naturally we're going to have to find some way of compensating the village that lost its food supplies.'

'Just one other thing,' Elliot asked mildly, 'what happens about their contract with U.C. — is that torn up too?'

'I don't know,' I said. 'But if you feel you've any lien on their services, I suppose you're free to take action in a civil court, if necessary.'

Elliot leaned forward and put a hand on my shoulder. 'I want to make a sincere appeal to you. In the first place I want you to know that I see your viewpoint and appreciate the fine job you're doing. After that I'm sure you'll realize that you're putting me in a bad spot over this contract deal. So all I ask you to do is to think again, and to think hard, before you do something that's going to have the effect of knocking down everything we've been trying to build up here. What's going to happen when the peones on the Project get the idea that they can scrap their contracts whenever they happen to feel like it? You know what's going to happen, don't you?'

I nodded with a kind of reserved sympathy.

'It's the end, so far as we're concerned. Just that — the end. We're finished. It means that a great and altruistic idea, years of planning and labour, and a hell of a lot of money are going down the drain. Thousands of men, women and children who had their feet set on the road to progress and enlightenment are going back to their witch-doctors, tuberculosis and starvation. I wouldn't like to think I was responsible for something like that happening, David. And for God's sake don't talk to me about action in civil courts. You've lived here long enough to know just how much good that would do us.'

I mumbled something indefinite. The passion in Elliot's voice had embarrassed me and taken me by surprise.

Elliot got up. 'Okay,' he said. 'I think we can leave it at that. Thank you for your patience in listening to me, and I still implore you to think about all the possible consequences before you commit yourself. We're all in it together here. I wouldn't want you to take this for anything it's not meant to be — I mean to say anything in the nature of a threat — but your future probably depends upon what happens here during the next few days, just as much as the Company's does. We're sitting on dynamite.'

'I know that,' I said.

He held out his hand and I took it and felt the fingers crack again.

'Be seeing you,' Elliot said, 'and don't forget to give it some thought.'

He went off and a moment later I heard the jeep start up and the radio come on. Then I went to my room and changed into civilian clothes, put my .25 Beretta automatic in my hip pocket, and went to look for Greta. Rather to my surprise she had already gone out.

I went through the public rooms and the garden looking for Greta, and then I wrote her an affectionate note telling her that I would see her in the early evening, if not before that, and left it for her with the reception clerk. After that I picked up Elliot's spare jeep and set out for Julapa.

For about twenty-five kilometres I was on the main road, going downhill all the way. Three kilometres from the village a trail branched off, and I had to leave the jeep and go on by foot. The trail followed a stream up through thick, tangled jungle. To the eye it was monotonous and without colour, but I always enjoyed a trip into the jungle because the hot smell of decay in the darkness of the underbush never failed to bring back my childhood to me, with something of the thrill and the mystery the tropical forest had held for me in those days.

As soon as I saw the position of the village I knew that Elliot's idea of surrounding it would have been out of the question, and for this reason they had probably built it in the position it was. Julapa was squeezed into a clearing under a horse-shoe of jungled cliffs. There was only one way in and one way out — along the trail I had come up, and when I got into the village the air trapped in this pocket under the cliffs was like warm syrup.

It was a squalid place — a jungle village that had grown up round a kernel of shattered magnificence. A great bronze bell lay half buried in the square, which was surrounded by roofless colonial buildings. Vigorous trees bearing fruit and flowers grew in the interior of a governor's palace. There were a hundred or so branch huts with hairless dogs and hairy pigs trotting in and out of them, and a market with women asleep at stalls selling rancid and fly-covered iguana flesh, gourds, cheap mirrors, sugar skulls and humming birds in paper bags for the children. Julapa was five-sixths Indian, just as Guadaloupe was five-sixths ladino, so the atmosphere was silent and brooding except round the church, which was the only stone building intact, where the Indians were praying in loud voices and swinging their censers. The whole place stank of ordure and decaying fruit.

Now I was here I hadn't any idea what I was going to do. I went round the village two or three times and looked into the huts. There were a few women about, their faces strained into a pretended indifference, and a few naked, malarial-looking children, but hardly any men. No one paid any attention to me. In dealing with strange whites the Indians have developed the simple self-protective trick of just pretending they aren't there. Somebody was tapping mournfully on the keys of a marimba out of sight, and mocking-birds hooted at me distantly from the cliffs.

I went into a blood-red painted cantina called 'The Little Chain of Gold', woke up the ladino patron, and bought a bright pink syrup-drink, strongly laced with aguardiente to knock out the worst of the germs. The patron didn't seem to want to talk. He kicked away the chickens from the place where he had been lying on the ground, lay down and went off to sleep again. I sat there over the warm, insipid drink, wondering what to do next. It was very hot. Flies came buzzing in and settled everywhere — on my face, my hands and the rim of the glass. I killed some and brushed them off the table on to the floor, and living flies dropped on the dead and dying ones and tried to couple with them. The cantina displayed one of the early benevolent pictures of the President, and there were the usual calendars presented by insurance companies, showing blonde girls with enormous, barely concealed bosoms — a form of art which is a source of great perplexity to Indians in places like this. There were a couple of heavy-calibre bullet holes in the wall close to where I was sitting.

I had been there perhaps half an hour when a fortune-teller with a canary came in. He collected two cents from me, put down the cage, opened the door and the canary hopped out on to the table top. The man took a little bundle of printed fortunes out of his pocket and put them on the table, and the bird nudged among them with its beak, picked one out, and hopped across the table to me, still carrying it. These canary fortune-tellers build a solid reputation by the simple device of making sure that there is nothing in the bundle but bad luck. After all, no villager could reasonably look forward to anything but poverty, sickness and disaster in one form or another, and what use would it be to promise an Indian unexpected legacies, success on the stock market, or journeys overseas? I opened the slip, while the fortune-teller watched me with a thin smile, and read, 'Thy beloved will leave thee'. Of course she would if I were a wretched Indian. She would die of malaria, leaving me with four motherless children, or of an infection after child-birth, or of any of a hundred easily curable diseases that keep the native population well down in a doctorless country. Or a ladino shopkeeper would dazzle her with his rings and chains and spirit her away. Or she would just get tired of life with a man who went off for six months at a time to work on a plantation, bringing nothing with him when he returned but the venereal disease and a few coins.

I got up, carrying inside me that small nagging credulity with which contact with superstition so often taints us, and I went to the church. It was a fine building that four hundred years of earthquakes had not shaken down, and I could see immediately that the Indians had taken it for their ceremonies — the Cuch-Cajans, or Calendar Priests as they are sometimes called, were standing guard by the doors swinging the copal censers. I went up to one of the Cuch-Cajans and bowed and asked permission to enter the church. He said nothing, but gave me a fierce look. As he made no attempt to stop me, which he would have done immediately had the church been barred to whites, I went in.

There were more Indians in the church than I had seen in the whole village, and from the varied costumes they were wearing I supposed that the church had been turned into a place of pilgrimage for many tribes. The immense interior was empty of furniture, but there were shrines all round the walls and the Indians were gathered in groups and semi-circles ceremonially dressed in a way you never saw them dressed in the streets, with head-scarves and long, tasselled shawls, and carrying their ritual bags. They were gathered round the clusters of candles they had lit and stuck into the shapeless masses of wax on the flagstones. Red blossoms had been strewn all round the candles lit for the souls of the living, and yellow blossoms for those of the dead. Many hundreds of candles were alight all over the great bare floor and they provided the only light in the church, which was without windows. The tribal prayer-leaders were standing or kneeling with the family groups and praying in those loud man-to-man tones the Indians use when addressing their gods. Here in the church the feeling was so different from the feeling you had in an Indian village that these might have been an entirely different race. The Indians here had come into their own.

Watching them, I wondered if there had ever been a people who had resisted as these people had resisted? The conquerors had come and had taken possession of them like human cattle. They had branded them to be held as slaves in perpetuity — they and their children — and had shared out all their young women among the soldiers. Rebellion had been punished with a repression that emptied whole countries of their populations, but still the Indians who survived held out. When the Church entered the battle it had fought at first with the Inquisition and the stake, and then, led by Bishop Las Casas — newly released from the madhouse where he had been driven by the horrors he had seen — it had returned to the attack with love. The iron-hearted politicians of the Church had put out their fires, dismissed their torturers and hangmen, and carried on the fight with kindness and toleration. Poor friars had gone into the mountains to spread the gospel-teaching, and the Indians had received them with gentle taciturnity and sometimes paid a little lip-service to the faith they preached. But in the end all had been in vain; the bloody slaughters and the devoted sacrifices alike. The Indians had remained aloof; and the silent gods of the rain, the corn and death had triumphed.

The Indians here, as in Guadaloupe, addressed their worship boldly and directly to the gods of their ancestors, and afterwards those who had held on to a little Christian practice as a measure of prudence placed themselves under the images of the saints to ask for their intercession with the Christian deity. I knew that the Indians thought of him as the god of the Judgment Day and Punishment, who stood between them and entry into the paradise of their forefathers. Some ladinos came here, too, and they had introduced a non-Indian principle into the many religious rites practised in this church, that of giving thanks for services rendered.

They had covered a wall with votive paintings offered in gratitude to San Felipe for benefits received at his hands. There were hundreds of pictures of all sizes, crowded together without method or order, all of them pathetic and some amusing. An electrician who had survived a severe electric shock was shown lying on the floor with lightning striking in all directions from his body. A woman who had come through a serious operation was on the table, and a surgeon with the face of a fiend stood over her, holding what looked like a pair of garden shears. A really beautiful scale drawing giving all measurements had been presented by an engineer who had fallen down a well, and he was shown being hauled back to the surface seated in a bucket, a smart ladino hat stuck squarely on his head.

I was taking in these details as well as I could in the yellow, smoky light when a high-pitched voice behind me said 'Good day, sir'. I turned with a start and a little man stood there, smiling up at me in a foolish way, his mouth half open. He had a dwarf's face, as smooth as a child's but age-less, and two or three long white hairs straggled out from under the point of his chin. His bones were like a wicker framework, jutting at shoulders, elbows and knees through the threadbare cotton of the shirt-like ecclesiastical garment he wore.

'Good day,' I answered. 'Are you the priest?'

'No, sir. There's no priest here. I'm the custodian of San Felipe. It's a hereditary position. We were allowed to stay here and look after the church when the priest went away because the saint took a liking to my family.' When he stopped speaking his mouth hung open, showing the tongue lolling just inside the lips. I realized that he was weak in the head, and imbecility had not only endowed him with a kind of macabre eternal youth, but had even smoothed out the differences of race in his face. He could have been anything, and although he was almost certainly an Indian, he showed not the slightest fear of me.

'Have you come to offer something to the saint, sir?'

I was embarrassed for a moment, not knowing what to say. 'I'll offer something if you like. What do people usually give?' I felt in my pocket, fumbling for a twenty-five or fifty cent piece.

'Has the saint cured you of a disease, or protected you from danger?'

'Well, I don't know — not that I'm aware of.'

'Then you may offer flowers. You can buy them at the door. Five cents is enough. The saint doesn't accept anything that costs a great deal. It's the mark of respect that counts.'

I went to the door with him and bought a bunch of blue flowers from the woman there for five cents, and then we went back into the yellow, incense-misted twilight to see the saint.

As I expected, it was an undistinguished piece of church statuary of the kind that workshops turned out by the thousand a hundred or more years ago, before the Faith had begun to relax its hold. The artist had gone to great pains with the carving of floating draperies, but his imagination had failed at the task of portraying sanctity of expression, and the result was insipid. The image was nearly black. This did not surprise me. The Indians could never quite persuade themselves of the loving kindness — even of a saint — with a white skin, so they usually contrived to put their images where incense smoke would darken them as soon as possible, or they even applied stain secretly to the exposed limbs. This saint had been turned into an Indian, humble, familiar and altogether reasonable in his demands, and even the purple and gilt of his draperies were covered with the friendly grime of smoke. What stood out so incongruously was the white cotton shirt over the dark torso. 'Why is he wearing the shirt?' I asked the gnome at my side.

'When an Indian is afraid of being killed he brings his shirt here, and the saint usually agrees to wear it. After that a bullet or knife can't touch him.' The gnome grinned broadly with pleasure at being able to answer my question so easily.

Something flashed in my head. 'And who left this shirt?'

The question was too direct. 'An Indian, sir. One of the Indians.' He would shrink quickly into a shell of cunning and subterfuge if I wasn't careful. 'The Indians are silly people, sir.'

'Is this the first shirt the saint has worn? In the last few days, I mean.'

The fixed grin twisted unhappily. He shook his head. From now on it would be a smoke-screen of evasion. The Indian would not lie in the presence of the saint, but neither would there be any way of getting the truth out of him. His sudden, stubborn obtuseness told me all I wanted to know.

I tried him from another angle. I cast doubt upon his miracle. 'But after all — between us two — a shirt can't save a man's life?'

He was mildly indignant. 'Yes sir, it will protect him while it is worn. When my father was a boy, before he became custodian, the Indians made a revolution and they brought their shirts here for the saint to wear, and the bullets wouldn't touch them.'

'And what happened afterwards?' I had never heard of a victorious Indian revolution.

'They were given all they asked for. Afterwards the soldiers came and took them away and hanged them, but they could not be harmed while they were wearing the shirts.'

Although everything was quite clear to me now, all I had really done was to confirm, to my own satisfaction, that the men I was looking for were really in Julapa, or hiding somewhere in the jungle around. I was no nearer than before to solving the problem of how to contact them.

I went out of the church and inevitably — because there was nowhere else to go — I strolled back to 'The Little Chain of Gold', thinking all the time about what was to be done. The patron was still asleep, where I had left him with the half-plucked, dusty-feathered chickens scrabbling round him. I was just going to shake him awake when I looked up and saw the benevolent picture of Balboa with that Let-Me-Be-Your-Father look of his, and the idea hit me.

I bent over the patron, took him by the shoulder and shook him, but not too hard, and then I looked out of the door, and there was not even a dog stirring in the sun. So I took down the poster and laid it on the table, and wrote in big letters across it: 'To the Chilams now hiding in Julapa, I, your father, President Balboa, promise pardon and freedom. Return immediately and bring in your arms.' I underlined some of the words like 'pardon' and 'freedom' several times, and then I added: 'You have nothing to fear.'

After that I rolled the poster up, pushed it down the front of my shirt and went over to the church again. The heat of the day was now on and the church was nearly empty. The candles had burned down and it had darkened inside and some of the Indians were sleeping on the floor. There was no sign of the gnome, so I went into the niche where they kept the saint and pinned the poster over the shirt.

There was nothing more to be done now. It was just after two o'clock, and the day was heavy and dull, with an almost equatorial heat. I went down to the cantina for a final drink, because I had been sweating a great deal and felt like drinking all the time. I had a couple of lemon syrups and was about to set out when I noticed that it was darkening so fast outside that it was almost like the lights going down in a cinema. One moment the sky had been colourless and heat-sodden as it always is in the afternoons in the tropics at this time of the year, and the next moment it was turning purple and I knew it would rain. It was weeks now since it had stopped raining in the highlands, but down in the tropics it was still the tail end of the rainy season, and at any moment the sky was liable to fill up with clouds, burst wide open, and let go a tremendous local deluge.

I stood at the door and watched the cliffs at the back of the village sink out of sight. When the first drops began to fall here and there it was like small, ripe fruits falling on the tin roof of the cantina. Then I saw a front of rain and lightning roll smoothly down on the village, and I sat there for two hours while the thunder charged round the cliffs, the rain hissed down, and the floor of the cantina became a shallow lake coated with drowned cockroaches. It was the heaviest downpour I had ever struck, and it made me think of the fate of the Spanish conquistadors in their first capital of Almalonga when the crater of the volcano Agua had filled with water, burst, and washed away the town below.

The rain stopped abruptly and the sun came through with a great prismatic dazzle of colour from the drops still showering from roofs and branches. The water was nearly ankle deep in the village and for the first mile the track was like a shallow stream. By the time I got to the main road it was drying quickly, leaving thin patches of mud here and there on the road's surface. The cushion on the jeep's seat was like a sponge. I squeezed out the worst of the water and threw it in the back, and I had just settled myself at the wheel when I noticed tyre marks in a patch of mud on the other side of the road. This struck me as extraordinary, because I would have said that you could have spent a week in a place like this without seeing a car pass.

The more I thought about it, the stranger this coincidence seemed to me. I turned the car round and went slowly down the road, following the tracks through the patches of mud. They started from the verge just round the bend. It didn't require any detective training to see by the crushed vegetation that the car had been parked among some bushes off the road, by the opening of a cave with a white fang of water in its black mouth. There were marks where the wheels had spun as it took off to climb the slight gradient, and you could also see where two men had come down the other side of the road and walked through the mud to get into the car. The tyre pattern and the width of the track were identical with that of the jeep I was driving, and it was quite clear that the other jeep had been parked where it was before the rains started and that it had been driven away after the water had drained off the road surface, probably only a few minutes earlier.

From the consideration of these facts I came reluctantly to the conclusion that I had been followed. But who had followed me? There were at least half a dozen jeeps in Guadaloupe and all certain to be fitted with the same make of tyre.

What was very much more to the point was why they had followed me — and what they had been able to discover?

By the time I got back Greta had gone. She had left a pencilled note, and the moment I saw the familiar slipshod handwriting on the envelope my heart sank, and I knew what to expect. 'Darling,' I read, 'they cancelled the flight on Thursday, and as I had the chance of a lift in a car most of the way to Coban today, I decided to take it. It was lovely as it always is to see you again, and as usual I wanted to say so many things that I never can say when the time comes' — at this point half a sentence had been carefully scribbled out — 'still I don't think you really have anything to say to me any more, so I thought there was no point in staying on any longer and making things worse for myself. Please forgive my being silly and sulky last night. I really had a wonderful time.' Reading this I could see Greta standing at the reception desk producing this last-minute scribble. She did everything without premeditation, and my one comfort at that moment was that just one look at Coban, which she hadn't seen since she left it as a child, would probably be enough to make her change her mind again.

14

_____

I F I could have found some way of putting off my lunch
with the Sterns, I would have done so. I was depressed
over Greta, and I did not feel like being obliged to make an
effort to be agreeable to people I didn't know very well.
That is to say I had lately spent about half an hour in Helmuth Stern's company when Elliot had also been present,
but I had not yet met his wife. Stern was U.C.'s archaeologist, and it was at least some consolation that we had an
interest in common.

The Sterns had built their house on a pinnacle overlooking
Guadaloupe and the view to anyone who was not sick of
tropical panoramas would have been extraordinary, but
Stern had had enough of the tropics. We stood at the picture
window — the whole side of the room slid open by pressing
a button — and looked down over the savage-coloured rocks,
the villages strangled in jungle, and over the fruit trees in the
garden suckling pale, parasitic blossoms, and Stern said:
'Do you know — I hate it. And that's not putting it too
strongly, either.' He smiled in a morose sort of way. 'This
room was Elliot's idea, but we stopped living in it after the
first few weeks. We take our meals in the kitchen where
there isn't a view except of some chicken-coops in the back-
yard.' Several glossy, crow-like birds settled on one of the
trees and shrieked and jabbered at us, and Helmuth rolled
his head from side to side in disgust. His wife, Lisa, a sweet,

cosy, faded little woman who looked as if she suffered from headaches, and exuded a fresh, clean smell like that of apples said: 'One can have too much of anything that's overdone, don't you think so, Mr Williams? We often think how nice it would be to get away for a month's holiday in Canada, where it is always cool and green and the people are so much more reliable.'

'And where there are no flowers,' Helmuth said. 'Or at least they are kept in their place. This stink of lilies everywhere is an intrusion on anyone's privacy.' Helmuth maintained an attitude of humorous embitterment. He was an Austrian who had got away a few weeks before the *Anschluss*, had spent a decade in Hampstead and the succeeding years in the colour, the sadness and the violence of Central America. Central America had brought out the European in him like a permanent facial rash.

'When we first arrived,' Helmuth said, 'our idea was to take what the tropics had to offer. In other words, to fit in. It looked like being here for good, so we were going to like it, whatever happened. Look at the house, it's like a permanent exhibition of native handicrafts. God knows, we tried.'

'We have some beautiful things,' Lisa said. 'There isn't room to show them all. When we were collecting I used to go out and buy the blouses the women were wearing in the markets. I used to carry plain blouses with me so that they could have something to put on. You don't see a lot of the designs any more, and the dyes they use nowadays are very inferior.'

'One of these days, I'm going to tear the whole lot down and make a bonfire of them,' Helmuth said with pretended ferocity. Lisa was gently and becomingly sad. It was hard to imagine her any other way, but a good half of Helmuth's attitude was a humorous pose.

'We used to go to parties on the fincas,' Helmuth said,

'but we found that we hadn't got any conversation. We didn't have any inside information about the President's mistresses. You're an intellectual in this country if you read *Newsweek*.' He sighed.

Somewhere below us on the flower-quilted mountain-side a bird began a powerful warbling. 'That's a guarda-barrancas.' Stern's sensitive face looked as if he had just detected a wretched piece of violin-playing in a Mozart symphony. 'It's supposed to be like the European nightingale — probably because it sings at night. When two or three of them get going at once, goodbye sleep. If it's not birds it's monkeys, howling like the souls of the damned.'

Lisa, who had gone into the kitchen, came back to say that lunch was served. The Sterns apologized for the food, which was certainly not good. It was impossible to get a cook: impossible to get any servant to do anything unless you were at her back all day long. There were no examples of Indian handicrafts in the kitchen, which was decorated with a photograph with an unnaturally dark sky taken by Helmuth of the Matterhorn, and some coloured pennants of the kind you buy at the top of Alpine passes. Lisa was a little miserable because the lunch had turned out worse than she expected.

After lunch Helmuth showed me some of the pieces he was working on from the excavations at Utitlan. He was cleaning them ready for the museum and they were of great beauty. One of the beakers was the most beautiful Old Empire piece I had ever seen, painted in greens, yellows and greys with feathered warriors and tribute bearers. It excited me to hold it in my hands. 'Tzakol?' I asked.

'Or early Tepeu.' Helmuth looked slightly startled. 'But how did you know? Do you go in for this kind of thing?'

'Some friends of mine used to deal in antiques.'

'You don't mean pre-Columbian stuff, do you?'

'Yes.'

'But that's illegal. You're not allowed to buy or sell that kind of thing.'

'I know. One of them got into trouble. They put him inside for smuggling antiques out of Mexico.'

'By God, they should have shot him. Probably a tomb-robber. Prison's too good for that kind of fellow.' Helmuth picked up the beaker with reverence. 'Beauty in it's highest form. Don't you agree with me? I don't know of anything produced by man that has a better claim to be described as great art.'

I agreed.

'I feel as though I understand the ancient Maya through the medium of this kind of thing. I've lived with it half my life and I never cease to marvel at it. They were a wonderful people. Do you know what they fell down on — the one thing they never succeeded in inventing that really matters?'

'Do you mean the wheel?'

'No, not the wheel. The wheel's not important. They never worked out a way of keeping their gods under control. The Europeans were smart enough to turn their god into a pretence, but the Mayan gods were the real thing. They took too much out of them. The Spaniards wouldn't have stood a chance if they'd arrived in the great period of the Old Empire. What can you say about a people with a stone-age culture who could work out a calendar more accurate than ours? Incidentally, have you been up to the ruins yet?'

'No. I was meaning to go.'

'I shouldn't. It's a waste of energy. You can read about the results of the dig in the monograph. U.C.'s bringing it out next month. That's all you want to know about it.'

Lisa, alert over her embroidery, rejoined the conversation as it dipped to a familiar level. 'Helmuth is very sad about the way the restoration was done. The Company did not follow his advice.'

'It was archaeological murder,' Helmuth said. 'Scientifically, I've been reduced to the level of a harlot.'

Lisa made a weak noise of protest. 'The Company have been very generous to us, Mr Williams, but I suppose they don't understand how a man like my husband feels towards his work. He takes his work very seriously.'

'It's like working for some half-crazy millionaire who's caught the culture bug. People think of these big companies as rational, unemotional affairs, but they're not. They're like silly, spoilt kids that get one enthusiasm after another. Today it's culture. Tomorrow it may be buying up a chain of newspapers, or starting a new film studio. I'm not a scientific archaeologist any more. I'm a company hireling. I've been made to feel dishonest.'

'It wasn't your fault, darling. You did what you could. It really wasn't Helmuth's fault, Mr Williams. They really did rather take advantage of him.'

'They had a lot of money to spend — that was the trouble; so they suddenly decided it might be nice to do something for the country. Mind you, the new tourist development craze of theirs may have had something to do with it, too. They must have had that up their sleeve for a long time. If only a tenth part of the funds had been available all would have been well. We should have excavated the place and left it at that. But U.C. wanted something spectacular. They wanted a nice reconstructed Mayan city for their money — something to compare with Uxmal or Copan. Do you know what Utitlan was like when we started work?'

'I was taken up there as a child. There wasn't much to see. All I can remember is a few mounds.'

'We cleared twenty-eight of them. It was a year's job. Elliot wanted to use bulldozers on the bush, but we couldn't let him for fear of damaging anything. It was the first time I'd been given a site all to myself and I wanted to do a perfect job on it. A few days after we had begun the actual digging into the mounds Elliot turns up with a fellow called Colethart who's supposed to be a restoration expert. I remember I was down on my hands and knees at the time, covered in dirt, scrubbing away with a toothbrush looking for inscriptions on a few feet of wall we had uncovered, and Elliot wanted to know what it was. I told him the truth. "I don't know," I said. "It could be anything."

' "Of course you know," Elliot says quietly. "It's your job to know, therefore you know." I couldn't make out whether he was joking or not. He was looking his usual amiable self. "I'm an archaeologist," I told him, "and whenever I can, I like to avoid guesswork. I might be able to tell you something more definite tomorrow, or in six months' time. On the other hand, I may never be any wiser than I am now. This city has been badly smashed up at some time — probably three or four centuries before the Spaniards got here." "All right," Elliot says, "let's put it this way. From your knowledge of the way these places are put together have you any idea of what this particular piece of stonework could be?" I was beginning to wonder what was on his mind. Just to humour him I said, "It might have been a wall of a ball-court." It was no use, by the way, trying to put him off with anything. I found out later he'd taken a short correspondence course in archaeology himself.

' "Good," Elliot says. "Oh, Mr Colethart," he says to his restoration expert, "I wonder if you would be so kind as to make a note of that." Colethart wrote it down. "Now," Elliot says to me, "what did you find under that big mound you've cut into over there?"

' "Vestiges of a pyramidal structure," I told him.

' "Do you mean by that it's some sort of a temple?"

' "It could be," I said. "It probably was."

' "What else could it have been?" he asks.

' "Almost anything," I told him, being absolutely frank. There's no point in pretending that we know more than a few relatively unimportant facts about these ancient sites. "For example," I said, "some authorities, like Morley, take the view that nunneries existed in the Old Empire, and if you subscribe to that theory it could have been a nunnery, or it could have been the palace of a high priest, or an observatory, or even a sacred pigeon-house. It could have been anything. It's almost certain we shall never know what it was."

' "In fact, it's all a bit vague, isn't it?" Elliot says.

' "I suppose it is," I told him. "Unless you have the good luck to find a dedicatory hieroglyph, these old Mayan structures tend to remain a mystery."

' "I see," he says. "Fine. That's what I wanted to know." He asked a few more questions, mostly technical ones, about the types of buildings put up at various epochs, and then he called Colethart over, and just for all the world as if he were asking a price for putting up a new warehouse he asked him to get down to producing an estimate for three temples and six public buildings. Colethart and I were to get together and decide what the buildings were to be; whether they were to be observatories, skull-platforms, vapour-baths, or what. It was a detail he didn't want to be bothered with.

' "That leaves nineteen mounds unaccounted for," I remember telling him. "What do you want done about them. Am I to go on with their excavation?"

' "Leave them for the moment," Elliot says, "until we see how funds stretch out. If we want a few more temples and ball-courts at a later date we can always have them. Or maybe we can level out the rest. We don't want to go and complicate things so that visitors get confused in their minds." What do you think of that?'

'I think it's fantastic,' I told him. 'Utterly fantastic. I can quite imagine how you felt about it. Didn't the Chilams have anything to say about it, by the way? I always thought the Indians were likely to turn nasty when this kind of thing

happened. After all, from their point of view you're dese-
crating the tombs of their ancestors.'

'That's what we were afraid of, too, especially when the
word got round and they came trooping in from all the
plantations with their aguardiente and their machetes. We
had police reinforcements rushed up from the city, but all for
nothing; they just sat about drinking and burning incense for
a bit, and then they went away. It was quite a let-down.'

Lisa said: 'We've given up trying to understand Indians
long ago. You never know what they'll do next. Our servants do the funniest things. You wouldn't believe some of
the things they do.'

'When you're dealing with Indians,' Helmuth said, 'things
never go the way you expect them to. Take these famous
bandits we're hearing so much about. If there's one thing
you can be quite sure of it's that they'll surprise you. I hear
there are more than a hundred of them hiding out in the
mountains now.'

'The latest figure I've been given is thirty odd.'

'All Elliot's Chilams, aren't they?'

'So far.'

'The Chilams,' Helmuth said, 'are an interesting survival
— a kind of racial coelocanth. As far as I know they're the
only tribe that escaped the Spaniards' clutches. That is to
say, they co-operated with them at first, and then when they
didn't like the way things were going they suddenly disappeared. They cleared off, complete with their priests or
shamans or whatever you like to call them, and they succeeded in hiding themselves somewhere in the mountains
where they stayed until the abolition of slavery — or should I
say the theoretical abolition of slavery? I expect you know
the kind of treatment Indians used to get from the planters.
And still get for that matter.'

'I've got a fair idea.'

'Elliot wants to do something with them. That's the latest

of his bugs. He's going the wrong way about it. I could tell him what to do. All he had to ask himself is, what keeps them together? What was it that kept them out of reach of the Spaniards' branding irons? Their religion, of course. Or in other words, their shamans. It's the shamans that Elliot is up against, but he doesn't seem to have found out yet.'

'I think he has,' I told him.

'It's the shamans he has to get rid of. After that he can do what he likes with them. They'll follow him like sheep. They wouldn't even know how to sow their maize if a shaman wasn't there to tell them.'

'And in the long run you think it would be the best thing for them?'

'Of course I do. As it is, they're nothing. They're totally negative. Elliot will get to work on them and do something with them. God only knows what the end-product will be like, but at least it won't be walking in its sleep. This is their ice-age as a race. They're finished and they have to change if they're to survive. Nobody ever changed themselves. Somebody has to do it for them from above, whether it's a priest with a new idea, or a king, or even a company.

'Do you know where all the shamans are?' I asked.

'Yes. Up on the top of Tamanzun.'

'Are they all up there? I mean to say, there aren't any more anywhere?'

'Not so far as I know.'

'In that case,' I told him, 'Elliot's problem's as good as solved. We're going to pick them up tomorrow.'

Helmuth's expression changed. 'You can't,' he said.

'Why not?'

'Well, I don't know — I suppose you can, but it's the kind of thing that could set off an uprising.'

'By whom? All the Chilams are safely under control in Elliot's concentration camp.'

'That's perfectly true, too, but it still sounds terribly risky to me. The least thing that can happen is that the shamans will jump into the crater as soon as anyone tries to touch them. They're worse than the Japanese for committing suicide. Can you imagine the outcry in Guatemala City?'

I was considering these unpleasant possibilities when a girl came in to take away the coffee cups. Helmuth suddenly bawled at her in Spanish. 'You still here? Didn't I tell you to go? Get to hell out of it!' He was really furious, and the sudden violence in this naturally mild man was rather shocking.

'I gave her the afternoon off to go to a fiesta,' he explained, 'but she won't go unless I shout at her and make a fierce face. They've got no conception of ordinary kindness and consideration as we understand it. You can't just give them something, you have to compel them to take it. I don't mind admitting that I've given up trying to fathom their mentality.'

A bird flew up and perched on the bars of the kitchen window and tittered insanely at us. 'And of course you have to allow for the fact that I hate the country,' Helmuth said.

'He needs a change.' Lisa gave him her weary little smile. 'A month or two in a cool country — somewhere like Canada — and he'd be a different man.'

15

I HAD never seen Elliot expansive in this way before. He wrung my hand and we got into his jeep. 'Glad you felt able to come along, Williams. It's a nice trip, and I guess that a nice trip's even nicer when it's shared.' Enthusiasm was running through him like an electric current. It was the first time I had seen him wearing a typical American holiday-maker's flowered shirt, and he had left off his tie.

The morning was as crisp and fresh as if it had just stopped raining, and all the colours were clean. We motored down out of Guadaloupe, the tyres sucking at the surface of the Company road, and then we turned off into the trail that went up to Tamanzun. The golden throat in the dashboard crooned at us softly. I couldn't understand what it was that was at the back of Elliot's gaiety. It made me feel uneasier than I had already been feeling at the prospect of this particular trip that we were now making together.

'Take a look at that view,' Elliot said. He stopped the jeep, pulled out a Leica camera and went and squatted by the roadside. The whole cone of Tamanzun had come into sight, remote and unreal, its flanks streaming mist and its summit wrapped in the morning turban of cloud that would soon be snatched away. The mist lay thicker at its base so that the whole mountain seemed to be floating above the surface of the earth. Elliot came back shaking his head. 'I guess I needed colour for that shot, but of course I had to leave my other camera behind.' He climbed into the jeep. 'I'm going to take up painting one of these days.'

We moved off, bumping gently ahead in second gear. Elliot was looking about him eagerly. He seemed to want to avoid any discussion of the business we had come on, and he drifted away from the subject when I brought it up. 'May as well take it easy,' he suggested, 'because otherwise we're going to get up there too darn soon. I figure it's a good hour and a half's ride for the men.'

'So long as we get there before anything starts,' I said.

'Oh sure. We'll see to that. Yes, as I was saying, art certainly is the thing to take your mind off your problems.'

I was waiting for Elliot to get round to the bandits, because there was no doubt at all that a panic had started in the town, but when he asked me how my investigations were going he did so in such an off-hand, perfunctory way that he might have been asking after the health of a distant relative. 'Oh fine, fine,' he said absently, when I gave him a guarded picture of my activities.

We were coming out of the last of the jungle now, and there were a few big ceiba trees, well separated, shading the trail, and Elliot suddenly pulled up with a jerk again and reached for the repeating shotgun he carried in a holster on the side of the jeep. I followed his aim as the gun went up, and saw a bird with a long tail swaying out on the end of a branch. Elliot fired, and the bird went straight up into the air and then dropped, and I heard the soft thump of its body hitting the ground by the side of the trail. It was a good shot. I should have said that the bird was out of range. Elliot came back with a drooping handful of colour. A membranous shutter slid back, revealed a bright eye, and closed again. Elliot poked a little loop of bowel protruding from the cloaca. back into position with his finger. '*Cotinga Amabilis*,' he said happily. 'I built up a nice little collection two years back.

Did a course in taxidermy, and I still don't like to pass up a chance like that.'

Elliot laid the dead bird tenderly on the back seat, re-cocked the gun, and put it back in the holster. He was genuinely happy. I was quite sure about it, and I wondered why I should find this, as I did, a trifle sinister.

'Do you sometimes get the feeling that a year of three hundred and sixty-five days isn't long enough? That's the feeling I often get. For my money a year of five hundred days would be about right, and even then I'd probably fall short of the programme I set myself most times. Do you know, I often feel sore when I think of the valuable time that goes down the drain eating and sleeping. I guess it's mostly my old man's fault. He had me tied to the farm until I was twenty-seven, and by the time I pulled myself out it looked to me like a pretty good slice of my life had gone without anything to show for it. I meant to ask you something — do you like hunting big cats?'

'Yes,' I told him, 'but it's a waste of time so far as I'm concerned. I've never had a shot at one yet.'

'I mention it because we're just passing the spot where I got a pretty nice mountain lion last year. You have to get yourself a good hunter if you want to get the cats. We have a ladino working in the dispensary at the Project who'll get you a jaguar every time you go out with him. I spent a whole year hunting cats with that character. I must have gone out hunting every night for a year. We got the cats all right. Some of those jaguars were as big as ponies. That was the year before I went in for aviation. I guess you and I will have to go out hunting the big cats one of these nights.'

'That would be fine,' I said. 'How are we getting on for time?'

'Oceans of it.' He glanced at his watch and seemed to remember something. He fumbled in the breast-pocket of his shirt, and then I saw his hand go up to his mouth. His Adam's apple slid up under his chin, and then dropped back into position. He felt my glance. 'These new co-pilots are all right,' he explained, 'that is to say, they don't dry up your throat, but the effect tends to wear off suddenly. I missed my sleep last night.'

At this point the trail suddenly steepened, and as Elliot found it necessary to engage the four-wheel drive, the wheels snatched at the layer of clinker that covered the trail. We were above the tree-level now, and the cone of the volcano that hung over us had come right out of the mist and was like iron. The trail was cut into the scalded slopes of clinker and ash that went sliding right down beneath us into the highest of the pines. Below that the jungle lay close-knit with a little breeze moving about in it, like muscles tensing and relaxing under a reptile's scales. A few bright, dove-plumaged vultures, the sun filtering through their wings, were swinging and turning overhead. Soon a crack opened in the landscape to give us a quick glimpse of Lake Tenyuchin, a dark hammock of water stretched between the distant peaks.

It was difficult to see what was happening at the crater when we arrived. I had half expected an open place, the dramatic terminal of the expedition, with figures silhouetted fatefully against the sky round the rim of an abyss — the typical film-setting of an unoriginal imagination. But here, where the mountain flattened off, there were smooth, black dunes and crumbling slag heaps, and the crater itself, when we found it, was like the black bed of a drained-out reservoir with a few tough bushes knotted into its slopes. The surroundings conspired beautifully to prevent you from seeing what, if anything, was going on. When we got to the end of the trail we were in time to see the last of the police going up to the crater, dumpy, untidy figures in bleached khaki uniforms, scrambling over the hillocks and then dropping out of sight as they went down the little gullies in the lava.

We also saw a single cavalryman leading his horse, but there were no Indians in sight.

When we couldn't force the jeep any farther into the clinker, we got out and walked. There was a strong, cool wind blowing round the slag heaps, so that Elliot's shirt and trousers were pulled tightly from his ribs, his shanks and his pelvis — which stuck out from the hollow of his stomach as if he were carrying a small, sharp-edged chair clasped about his hips. He was as agile as a mountain goat over the terrain, although the height of this volcano is 13,103 feet, and at that height your muscles lose half their power and your breath comes as if you had just finished a hundred yards' sprint. 'Where do you suppose all those characters can have hidden themselves?' he asked. He skipped up a hummock of lava and I went after him heavily, filling my shoes with sharp-edged cinders. Somewhere, hidden from us in this infernal landscape, I had a vision of the Indians making a last stand; then taking refuge in their honourable custom of mass suicide by throwing themselves into the crater — although I later found that this particular crater would not have been suitable for that purpose.

When, in the end, we discovered one of the shamans, nothing dramatic was happening. Two policemen, one of whom looked like a boy of sixteen, were dealing with him. The older policeman was laying down the law in a disgusted fashion, with a great spreading of hands and a hunching of shoulders, as if he were reprimanding a drunk he had caught washing his clothes in the public fountain. The young one, bent slightly under the weight of a huge old Mauser rifle strapped across his thin shoulders, looked on with an embarrassed smile.

The old Indian stood with his back to his altar, turning his head from side to side and standing first on one foot and then the other. He wore a thick, black cape; his thin, inward-curved shins stuck out of the usual knee-length breeches, and there were big, open sores on his hands and feet, of the kind which are common enough among old Indians who don't get enough to eat. Elliot was interested in his hat. 'Well, for heaven's sake — take a look at that headgear.' It was like a pale grey Edwardian bowler with a huge, curling brim and it was stuck squarely over his head, coming right down to the eyes. The Indians love hats. They are humble, but their hats are proud. They are the hats of the white men and they symbolize the power and the intelligence of the conqueror. You could see nothing of this Indian's face, which had been blotted out entirely by many thousands of wrinkles, and even the eyes were nothing more than two small wrinkled whirl-pools just under the brim of the huge, arrogant hat. He must have been a hundred years old.

We stood there while the older policeman laid down the law and the young policeman grinned vacantly and the old Indian's head went from side to side as if he were looking for some last-moment intervention on the part of whatever gods he served on the bare mountain-top. Then the discussion seemed to come to an end. The young policeman re-slung his gun more comfortably and went off, with the old shaman following him, and his colleague began to kick down the altar. The altar was no more than a heap of stones, about five feet high, with pieces of rough, broken pottery piled on top. The old Indian didn't look back at the policeman kick-ing his altar to pieces and he was soon out of sight. There was an opening in the stones at the bottom of the altar with a blackened censer in it, and Elliot picked it up and handed it to me. 'This any interest to you?' I shook my head. 'Crude, isn't it?' Elliot said. He threw the censer away, and it smashed against a rock.

'I thought there might have been an idol or two up here. You ever seen one of their idols?'

'Only in a museum,' I told him.

'They're pretty crude too, but I could have used one in

the vestibule of the Mayapan. I figure a legitimate idol would look pretty effective there. A touch of the right atmosphere.'

But as it turned out there were no idols on Tamanzun — only rough stone altars and a lot of fire-blackened pottery. The police went round and kicked the altars down and took the shamans away — a small, limping procession of six old men in grand hats. The whole thing was over in an hour without shouting or violence, and then Elliot and I went over to inspect a place where he had decided to build what he called a mountain refuge, and Elliot threw further light on the day's operation.

We went to the edge of a small plateau on which an alpine café would shortly be built and looked down on Guadaloupe — a crystalline sparkle of buildings with the roads coming into it like the broken spokes of an old wheel.

'Now would you have supposed that those old guys were at the bottom of all the trouble we were having?' From the tolerant, almost affectionate way Elliot said 'old guys', I knew that he was sure he had won a big victory.

'A bunch of old scarecrows like that! Can you imagine that they had some sort of bush telegraph system going with our people in the Project, telling them what to do and what not to do? That's why we were getting the desertions. That's why people were refusing to have their injections, and refusing to worship in the church we put up for them. Who do you think put the finger on them in the end?'

'Miguel,' I said. It sounded improbable, but I couldn't think of anyone else.

'Right.'

I thought about Miguel, and his character baffled me. My guess would have been that he would have been beyond the effective range of pieces of silver. 'A bit of an old Judas,' I said, 'after all.'

Elliot considered this verdict with a judicious pursing of the lips. 'As I've said before, he likes whisky. That comes very expensive for an Indian, so I guess he wants to go right on being mayor, rather than sign up as a peon and stop drinking whisky. Not that he thought we could do anything about it. We weren't the first to try to get rid of the old chaps. Maybe he didn't think we could touch them either.'

I brought up the matter of the so-called bandits and Elliot shrugged his shoulders.

'I'm not bothered about them. We've stopped the leak. That's what matters. Anyway, I'm relying on you to take care of that side of the deal.' He grinned. 'I've got a lot of confidence in your methods, David.'

A few minutes later we passed my cavalrymen, bored and sleepy-looking in their saddles, their horses picking their way delicately down the loose-surfaced slope; and then we came up with the shamans going down the hill in single file in their normal shambling dog-trot, the police on each side, rifles carried at the trail.

'What happens to them?' I asked Elliot.

'Oh, I don't know. Nothing much, I suppose. Maybe we can manage to keep them out of circulation for a while. The processes of justice can be pretty slow in these countries.'

He turned the knob in the dashboard a little and a saxophone whined urgently. A few minutes later we were in Guadaloupe.

We hadn't gone a hundred yards along the street that leads into the Calle Barrios before I knew that there was something wrong. It was the time of day when the shopkeepers would put up their shutters, change quickly into clean, well-pressed suits and saunter down to the plaza for three or four turns round the Liberty monument before going home to lunch. But today the place was deserted, and there was something in the atmosphere that reminded me of Guatemala City just before the fighting had broken out between the Army of Liberation and the regulars.

Halfway up the Calle Barrios I saw an armed man ahead of us. He looked like an extra in the film about Zapata. 'Hold on,' I said to Elliot, 'what on earth's that?'

'Where? — oh him. He must be a vigilante.' Elliot was cheerful and showed no signs of surprise. 'I heard they were forming. Kind of irregular militia. Always liable to appear on the streets when they get the idea there's any trouble in the wind.'

'Indeed,' said I. 'Let me get out.'

—————

16

Eʟʟɪᴏᴛ put me down and I went after the man, although I had no clear idea of what I was going to do when I caught up with him. The fellow was shuffling along a dozen yards ahead of me. He was almost certainly one of the desperadoes who had appeared on the scene in the last few days, and I was afraid that the cartridge bandolier and the Mauser slung on his back had come out of the town armoury. The street had gone blind in the sun; all the doors and windows closed and barred; juke-boxes in two of the cantinas were playing songs by the Mexican Jorge Negrete, turned up to full strength, filling this part of the town with a muddled, nostalgic roaring; a dog on its haunches was howling out in the middle of the empty plaza.

I turned the corner out of the square with the so-called vigilante just ahead, and then he was gone. Now there was nothing moving at all in the street, and it was shadeless and glittering in the hard midday light. I stopped and looked round me, and then I thought of the cantina 'Thou and I' which was in this street, although too far ahead for the man to have reached it before I turned the corner. When I got to the cantina I looked in over the swing doors, and then I went in. I was on good terms with the bartender here, and once or twice in the past he had intervened to prevent his customers from picking quarrels with me. The place was empty and the bartender was in his usual position. I was expecting a welcome of some kind from him, but he looked away from me and over my shoulder. His face had gone tight and he seemed to have shrunk, and while I waited for the smile that didn't come I heard the soft flop of the swing doors behind me. I turned round and the ladino, who had evidently realized he was being followed and had decided to turn the tables on me, was there.

The moment I saw the squinting look on this man's face I knew he was going to kill me if he could. The bartender's expression would have told me that anyway. But the ladino was too late. I was facing him now, and for all his armoury he was paralysed with embarrassment. He stood there twisting his hands, his mouth screwed up into a sheepish smile. He had missed his chance in not shooting me from the door when my back was turned, and now that we were face to face he could not kill me in cold blood. I recognized this man as a frontier-jumper who probably lived from the receipts of occasional robberies — the kind of man who was supposed to be ready to kill an Indian for ten dollars or a ladino for twenty. He was a drunkard and a marihuana smoker like all such types, but he had his ladino standards and it was proper and decent to stab in the back, a man with whom you had no particular quarrel, or to shoot him from an ambush. But to kill such a man standing face to face it was first necessary to provoke him into a display of insulting conduct, and thus provide the justification. As a murderer the ladino tough suffers under the handicap of an inbred politeness, and this has been his undoing in many a frontier affray fought with the Yankee gunfighters of old, who observed a different trigger etiquette. I recalled this while the vigilante moved round me towards the bar, his face wearing its silly expression, and, as he passed I pivoted slowly to keep my face to him. 'A very good afternoon,' I said.

'And a good afternoon to you, sir.'

'Would you care to join me in a drink?'

145

The ladino's embarrassment deepened. If he wanted to find an excuse to kill me any courtesy that passed between us would make this more difficult. A nervous twitch caught at the skin at the side of his eye. 'In my opinion,' he said, 'you don't wish to drink with an uneducated person like myself. As I see it, everyone has a right to his privacy.'

'Nonsense,' I said heartily. I ordered aguardiente and the bartender put down a bottle with two glasses and two saucers with salt. He didn't want to look at either of us. I wondered if he kept a sawn-off shotgun under the counter, in western movies style. The situation was pure old-fashioned horse opera. It was straight out of one of those ancient westerns that a travelling cinema would put on most Saturday nights in all the country towns of Central America, using the church wall as a screen. I knew that the ladino would be a keen student of this kind of cinematographic art and would try to model his actions along the general lines of conduct laid down.

I raised my glass, leaned over and resolutely clinked it against the one the ladino had taken uncertainly in his hand. We both drank, then correctly sprinkled a little salt on to the backs of our hands and licked it off. 'I repeat,' said the ladino, 'that some gentlemen prefer their own company. And well, why not? They have a right to it. You, for instance, might well not wish to be seen in the company of a person — well, let's say of small education — like myself. You must admit that.' The muscular spasm extended its range, caught at his eye and closed it. The other eye peered at me closely through narrowed, mongoloid lids. I didn't like this increasing nervousness on the ladino's part. I was just going to fill his glass again when he took the bottle out of my hand and said with a bitter smile, 'I see that we are drinking the cheapest aguardiente to be found.' It was Santa Margarita, an illicit local distillation, strong and raw, and about ten cents a bottle cheaper than the *nacional*, which paid a liquor tax.

'I was under the impression,' I said, 'that you gentlemen had a preference for something with a bite in it.'

'When you say "you gentlemen" what is that supposed to include?'

'Well, in a broad manner of speaking . . .' — I hesitated and searched for a palatable description for the cut-throats that spent half their lives in such places as 'Thou and I'; I also remembered at that moment that many ladinos refused to admit their possession of mixed blood — '. . . Well, let's put it men who lead an open-air life.'

'You mean the shelterless poor, who have only their pride in which to wrap themselves.' The ladino's twitch had ceased. He was beginning to see a way out now, and he backed away a little to give himself more room for action. I was wondering urgently when my mounted patrol would pass and how long I could delay inflicting the fatal wound on the susceptibilities the ladino had bared so hopefully.

The glass tinkled on the floor and the ladino looked distastefully at the small pool of liquid spreading into the pine needles. He picked the bottle up and inspected the label sourly. 'This stuff isn't for gentlemen; it's for cabrones.' At that moment the door behind us swung again, slicing at us with sharp bars of shadow. I followed the ladino's glance and saw another vigilante standing there, complete with Mauser, pearl-handled pistol in shoulder-holster and machete hanging from his hip. He took off his hat, bowed twice and advanced on us with a ferociously ingratiating display of yellow teeth. The ladino at the bar put down the bottle and returned his salutation with courtesy that might have been of the kind exchanged by provincial governors at the Viceroy's audience. The newcomer picked up the aguardiente and his expression softened. 'Ah, Santa Margarita, I see. Do you permit me, gentlemen?' He reached for a glass, filled it and swilled down the liquor, choked happily, licked the salt off his hand, and looked round. 'Why no music?'

There was an enormous juke-box in the corner with a kind of miniature puppet theatre fixed up on top of it, and above that a shrine with faded flowers and a lighted candle. The second ladino went over to the juke-box and smoothed its glossy flanks with reverent hands. 'Well gentlemen, I have to admit it, I can't read.' He looked back at us and gave a rueful shake of the head. 'If either of you could assist . . . the fact is I'm an admirer of "Far-Away Bliss" sung by Negrete. If that's not on the list "Mortal Sin" would do just as well.'

I exchanged a nod of understanding with the first ladino and we moved over together to the juke-box. 'Far-Away Bliss' was on the list and the second man put a five cent piece in the slot and both of them edged forward, studiously casual, but anxious to watch the reptilian mechanical gropings within the machine by which their choice of records was singled out and manœuvred into the playing position. The curtains of the marionette theatre jerked back, the small dusty marionettes composing the toy orchestra bent over their instruments, a huge electrical purr filled the cantina, and Jorge Negrete began to sing. Both men reached at once to turn up the volume and every object in the room was united in a great, tingling vibration. The marionettes jigged and fiddled and Negrete hoarsely implored a little water from the pitcher of someone's love. The pick-up arm crept over the spinning surface towards the dangerous silence at its centre, and I tried to calculate how long it would be before my men came trotting past on their way back from the volcano, and wondered whether I should hear the hoof beats through these vast tides of sound. 'It is a composition of the greatest beauty,' the second ladino shouted. 'I do not think it could be bettered. Perhaps when it is finished we should play it again.'

'For my part I prefer the same singer in his rendering of "Maria Dolores",' the first man bawled back. 'But whether

148

it is in the list is another matter.' He bent forward to peer uncomprehendingly at the list, and the handle of an old-fashioned pistol protruded from his hip pocket.

'It is,' I told him. I was ready with a coin. Both men edged closer to the machine again to watch the new record taken in the mechanism's stealthy embrace and lifted into the playing position.

The needle crackled in the ruined grooves, the familiar tiger's breathing filled the saloon, and someone began to pluck at the chords of a cosmic guitar. The bodies of the ladinos sagged, losing their angularity as the music poured into the great emptiness of their souls. Their movements became drugged. The second ladino's fingers caressed the juke-box's flowing surfaces as if it were the form of his beloved.

I backed away from them gently and reached the door, and at that moment I saw the first of the horsemen come round the corner. I stepped out and they saw me.

The vigilantes were still floating above the earth's surface, cradled in a tremendous cacophony of guitars, when soldiers rushed in on them and took their guns away. Sergeant Calmo, happy and ferocious, stood them against the far wall, hands on heads. He came back through the low swing doors and saluted. 'At your orders, Captain.'

'Ask them why they are carrying arms in contravention of martial law,' I told him. I knew that I was not going to like this. I went in again after him. In response to the sergeant's nod the bartender went over to the juke-box and cut off the spate of sound.

'Why are you carrying guns, mother-besmirchers?' The sergeant put his question in the unnaturally quiet tone they always seemed to favour in interrogations conducted in this country. He hardly reached the ladino's shoulder.

The ladino with the facial spasm winked at him morosely. He did not reply.

'I addressed a question to you, mother-besmircher.'

'And I heard you, sonny-boy.'

'Hit him.'

One of the cavalrymen clumped across the floor, measured the distance and swung at the ladino's face. He, too, was shorter than the ladino and he had to reach up to deliver the blow. The ladino did not appear to notice what was happening.

'Why are you carrying guns?' Calmo asked in a friendly voice.

The ladino's affected eye opened again. 'Do you wish to know my family name?'

'Why?'

'Because it would permit you to address me properly, sonny-boy.'

'Hit him again,' Calmo said. 'Several times.'

The cavalryman, who was smiling broadly, took up position in front of the ladino and began to swing with both fists, very unscientifically, striking at the head. I was on my guard against the sickness that might take me by surprise if I allowed this sight to affect me. Calmo turned to me in a kind of gentle bewilderment. 'The mother-besmircher simply doesn't want to talk, Captain.' The ladino's head swivelled from side to side under the weight of the blows. 'Good,' I heard Calmo say, 'and now let's try again.'

The ladino rocked back into the vertical position like a fairground Aunt Sally. He hooked with a finger in his mouth and took out a tooth, staring at it with affection and also a kind of surprise, as if it were something of value he had discovered in a sea shell. He smiled stiffly with half his mouth and bowed a little. 'If you wish me to answer your questions, kindly address me properly,' he said.

This man, I decided, was still playing his part in a western melodrama. More and more in these countries real life situations tended to mould themselves along the lines established by movie models. Besides which, his wits and his senses would be deadened by marihuana.

Sergeant Calmo drew his revolver and held it butt uppermost. He paused, looking round for a heavier weapon. The second ladino stopped licking his lips and joined in. 'My friend wants to co-operate with you, gentlemen. I'm quite sure of that. If you could perhaps extend a little more consideration . . .'

'Horse-abuser,' the sergeant turned on him. 'Who spoke to you?'

'Leave him,' the first ladino said, 'and remember the saying that if pigs could walk on their hind legs all soldiers would grunt.'

They were all watching him. The bartender had brought out his young children to watch the spectacle, and you could almost feel the eagerness of the soldiers. The sergeant picked up a bar stool and the muscles tightened in my stomach. I knew that the slightest sign of squeamishness or compassion would finish me as the leader of these men. The nausea was coming and going like a pulse, but I was determined to fight the weakness and I put into action my new mental trick.

I tried to concentrate on the true insignificance of individual suffering weighed in the scales against the ocean of pain being inflicted in the world at that instant. At that very second a thousand children were trapped in secret places at the mercy of rapists, ten thousand women writhed in the final agonies of death by childbirth, a million cancer sufferers screamed. Victims of the mad logic of the old religions that still had a third of humanity in their grip were being circumcised, infibulated, cicatrized and flogged for the love of God. Men, women and children were dying by the hundreds of napalm, bullets and bayonets, in small, unpublicized wars and risings. Exemplary action was being taken in Africa, social readjustments were going on in China, and the police everywhere were devising new and ingenious means of eliciting truth. This man's suffering was no more than a single atom in an expanding universe of affliction.

The second man was quite ready to answer questions when the sergeant threw down the bar stool. 'The Indians were coming, so naturally they had to look round for persons of integrity and spirit to defend the town.'

'What Indians?' I said. 'What are you talking about?'

'The bandits, sir. According to the reports they're terrorizing the countryside. An appeal was made to our honour as responsible citizens. Naturally we couldn't refuse. They gave us the guns and a small sum to cover expenses. We felt that lives and property, not to mention the honour of our women, were at stake.'

'Yes, yes, of course, but where are the rest of them? Didn't you say there were thirty or forty of you?'

'They're at Julapa, sir. They took them away in the trucks to fight the bandits.' The man on the floor started to get up. He coughed and spat out a little blood. 'I was detained searching for my friend,' the second ladino added. 'He is much addicted to alcohol and gets into trouble if left to himself.'

17

YOU have to know only a few simple facts about the Indians' mental background to be able to predict the way they are likely to act in given situations. In the first place it is essential to know that important actions of any kind are undertaken only on one of their lucky days. This applies to all Indians of Mayan stock who observe the ancient calendar with its twenty-day month. It has nothing to do with astrology or horoscopes, but is almost certainly the legacy of some genius of the Old Empire with a mania for statistics.

The day of the incident with the two ladinos was remarkable to the Indian mind not only because it was lucky — 'Spirit of Ancestors', by name — but because it had been preceded by three unlucky days in a row: 'Intelligence', 'Trouble maker' and 'Unknown', and it would be followed by another day of evil omen: 'Come Forth'. These were facts which I had overlooked. That is to say, although I knew something of the sequence of good and bad days in the Indians' calendar, I had never considered their possible application to the present crisis. Later, on giving some thought to the way the situation had developed, it became clear that someone else had been more alert. Whoever it was had collected the so-called vigilantes and sent them down to Julapa had chosen his moment in a most intelligent manner.

In deciding to accept the President's offer of a free pardon extended through my agency, the Chilams timed their action almost exactly as this person had foreseen, being at the most a few hours late for the appointment he had arranged for them with death. They started out at midday, some six hours after an ambush had been set for them by the vigilantes about a mile below the town, half-way down the trail to the main road where I had left the jeep. Here the stream and the trail that followed it passed through a narrow ravine, and a series of landslides following the heavy rains had up-rooted and swept away the thick vegetation that would have offered cover in an attack. By sunrise the vigilantes were comfortably in position among the rocks and trees above the landslides. It seems that their discipline began to wear thin in the six hours of waiting, but it is also clear that the Chilams had no idea of what was in store for them as they came hurrying in twos and threes down the trail in their characteristic trotting walk.

The organizing genius in the background, whose identity I could only begin to suspect, had followed classical models in the laying of his plans; insisting, so far as could be gathered, that the Chilams be allowed to pass through the narrowest part of the defile — which was then to be blocked behind them — before the massacre started. As soon, in fact, as their victims were safely through the bottle-neck, the vigilantes hidden with the Browning machine-gun at the top of the slope were to open fire. According to theory the whole thing should have been over in a couple of minutes.

It emerged, however, from my subsequent investigation, that the target presented by the Chilams was considered a disappointing one. Instead of coming into sight in a conveniently compact body, they dribbled past in twos and threes with long intervals between each group. An argument is supposed to have arisen among those who awaited them with levelled guns whether to fire at the front, the middle or the rear of the party, and it came out clearly that the man who actually fired the machine-gun had never fired one before and had no experience of its mechanism. Leaving out all these factors, it is a solid fact that nothing is easier than to miss a sitting target with a modern machine-gun, as I have discovered for myself when I once fired at a gazelle in the Western Desert at a range of thirty yards with a Spandau stripped off a crashed German plane. At all events, the Browning opened up, fired a hesitant burst, and promptly jammed, and the Chilams scattered and hid among the big boulders in the bed of the stream. The vigilantes spread out to surround them, but in this way they lost contact and very soon they were shooting at each other.

By the time we came upon the scene about four hours later, the situation — as they say in military circles — was confused. I was on horseback with the sergeant out in front of the patrol, aching already from the long unaccustomed ride, and we heard shots, which may or may not have been fired at us, whipping through the trees. We dismounted and took cover behind some rocks. It was here that we picked up a vigilante who had been nicked in the collar-bone by a bullet and had had enough of the battle. From what he told us, I gathered that the vigilantes had gone wild with fright and were shooting at anything that showed itself. He also mentioned that the story had got round that the Indians couldn't be touched by bullets, and that this had proved very demoralizing. Religion, as far as these town ladinos went, was never much more than a matter of wearing medals of the saints, but they went after superstitions like crows after scraps of bright cloth. I doubted whether any of them would be able to take steady aim after hearing about the magic shirts.

The captain of this expedition, said the ladino, was one Morales, who had recently been let out of prison after serving a five-year stretch for banditry. Unfortunately the breech had blown out of Morales' vintage Mauser, carrying away most of his face; and this man and another, who had bolted in a different direction, had been dragging Morales to the rear when they had come under fire. As the shooting had stopped again, we went forward, leading the horses, and soon we found Morales where they had left him. He was dead all right, and a great number of butterflies on the side of his face obscured the details of what the bolt had done to him. The butterflies were crowding, packed in layers like a swarm of bees, with their wings closed and barely flickering. A patch of blood-wetted dust under Morales' head was likewise coated with butterflies, so that it appeared to be resting comfortably on a multi-coloured pillow.

We moved Morales' body to the side of the trail where the long grass covered it; at that moment the firing started again and with a great deal of effort I got the soldiers down behind cover. Their particular superstition was that courage was invulnerable. Given half a chance they would have got up and walked calmly and without haste towards the guns; the hard task was to control them without letting them suspect how differently I felt about these things. The sound of shots went charging and crashing all round the ravine.

This place, I observed, was full of animals. It was a beautiful place for anything but a battle. I could hear startled animals, which I presumed to be wild pigs, come crashing down through the undergrowth towards us, and then, when only a few yards away but still invisible, catching our scent and turning off. The handsome white vultures of the kind I first noticed on Tamanzun were here, too, circling over the valley ahead of us but prevented by the shooting from dropping down on whatever it was they saw. Strangely enough it was not the vultures but the butterflies that made me feel uneasy. They were hovering about us; each man had his little attendant cloud of them. I was reminded of the inexplicable instincts that various insects are supposed to possess.

I lay behind a boulder as big as a small house trying to encourage a sense of security. This boulder might have been in its present position for a thousand years. A small separate jungle covered its top, and thick moss and ferns were growing down its sides. The trail curved round the boulder and after that came into the open, where it was like a railway cutting, with the stream and the trail at the bottom, and the landslides coming smoothly down to them, and no cover. The landslides were about a hundred feet in depth — fresh, red earth with a few uprooted trees sticking out of it. A few feet above the level where they started the ravine suddenly widened out and the jungle started, overhanging the slope a little in the manner of a heavy quilt laid on a divan bed. Having summed up these topographical facts, my plan was to do all I could to stay just where we were until sundown when I supposed that the shooting would stop and, in a manner of speaking, everyone would go home. We still had two hours to go.

In this lull I gathered some nervous strength and felt the cautious beginnings of confidence for the outcome. Thinking about the Chilams I felt at that moment that in extricating them from their predicament, if it could be done, I should be performing an action of value for the first time in my life. In the light of this moment my past existence seemed to me always to have been dedicated to triviality. At this stage I was slightly exhilarated by danger, as if from an ice-cold bath, and when Sergeant Calmo, who was reconnoitring, hissed to draw my attention I got up and went to him out in the open. We stood out in full view of the whole valley, and I was sure that I felt at ease. 'Over there,' Calmo said.

I followed the direction of his finger, but I couldn't see anything unusual. All the outlines were crisp now with the approach of evening. A curtain of shadow thrown down by the hills was creeping down the road towards us, and there were many objects in the valley to take the eye. 'I don't see anything,' I told him, and as I spoke something white flickered among the rocks in the bed of the stream, very much closer than I had expected to see anything move. While I looked there was another movement in a different position. Two white-shirted figures came into sight for perhaps two seconds, and then dropped back among the boulders. 'The Chilams,' Calmo said. 'They seem to be collecting behind that big egg-shaped rock. I do not think the cabrones can see them from the top.'

This new development, I thought, was a bad thing from my point of view. While the Indians were split up in twos and threes they were more or less safe in a negative kind of way. They would never act as individuals, but when they came together they were apt to develop a kind of corporate mind which was capable of taking decisions to which every member of the group would blindly adhere. 'I'm afraid that this means they may be coming out,' I told Calmo.

'Yes. As soon as they are all together, I think they will advance.'

'They've a good two hundred yards to cover. I can't see many of them getting here alive.'

'If the machine-gun the cabron spoke of functions once more — not one, I think.'

'Which means that we must act before they do.'

'I agree with you, Captain, that quick action would be a good thing.'

'And what do you propose?'

'Well, Captain, I think we should go and fetch them.'

'We'd never get there. They'd pot us off like rabbits.'

I couldn't interpret Calmo's look. 'I think you're right, Captain. With your permission I'll go by myself.'

'And then?'

'I'll keep them in their present position until dark, and then bring them in.'

Bravery can be a kind of addiction. I always suspect the very brave of being constantly on the look-out for opportunities to prove themselves — to offer sacrifices to a very dangerous kind of vanity. I therefore examined the proposal with suspicion, but could think of nothing better to offer in its place. In a voice that was not my own I said: 'I'll come with you.'

'I don't think that would be a good idea, Captain.'

'And why wouldn't it be a good idea?'

'I don't know how to explain. You have to show a great deal of confidence in front of these cabrones. I would feel happier if I were by myself.' What was really at the back of his mind, although he wouldn't say it, was that not being a vaquero meant that I didn't possess that special courage that conferred invulnerability.

'All right,' I told him. 'Go by all means. If you get there — and I'm sure you will — my orders are that you're to keep under cover till nightfall, and then we will come down and relieve you.' We shook hands, and I felt a great deal of affection for the man. 'You're not taking your horse?' 'No,' he said, 'I'll go on foot.'

I didn't like that at all. That, I thought, was a very bad sign. It meant that he wasn't willing to risk the animal, and I knew that when the vaqueros found themselves in a bad jam they would always risk their lives to save their horses. I'll give him a silk shirt, I thought, if he comes through this. It was the only gift that I could think of that would have any appeal for a vaquero.

'Hasta luego, Capitan,' he called, turning round to wave as he set off up the trail. At least that sounded better. If he had really thought that he was committing suicide he would have said Adiós. I had the soldiers cover him with their rifles as well as they could, but it would not really have been much use, because beyond the fact that the vigilantes were hiding up in the underbrush, we had no idea of their position. Calmo had left his gun and his pistol behind, and on my orders he was carrying a stick with a white handkerchief tied to it. It was a theatrical performance. A few butterflies fluttering after him, he sauntered down the path passing out of the sunshine and into the shadow, stopping to look around him and to slash the heads off flowers with the stick from which the handkerchief had quickly become detached. He waved again and we all waved back, and some of the men shouted. I was beginning to count the paces, thinking of the forty assassins in ambush at the top of the slope; alcoholics, paranoics, victims of marihuana and their own hatreds, men who would kill for the sheer amusement of it, watching over the sights of their rifles while a man who had made many enemies, a representative of detested authority, of the government that had starved and beaten them in prison, walked quietly by. You had to remember that this was a battle, and if Calmo had fallen it would never have been known who had fired the shot. So I counted the slow paces until he left the path and began to climb down into the bed of the river and I could only see the top half of his body. And then, at last, he was out of sight, and this time we all shouted, and the vigilantes up in the jungle whistled and shouted back at us.

Now that Calmo had got through safely to the Chilams I could see no justification for the rest of us hanging back, and I was just about to give the order to mount when one of the horses bolted. Startled, most likely by a snake, it tore loose and went charging away into the undergrowth and up the side of the hill, and firing broke out immediately. From this firing we learned surprisingly that there were some vigilantes on our flanks, as well as ahead, and that they were uncomfortably close. The horse may have passed near a vigilante who, taking it for a tapir — which are numerous in these parts — would have been likely to take a sporting pot-shot at it. But whether this was so or not the shooting set off a chain reaction and several bullets whined off the rocks behind which we were lying, causing me to abandon my intended action, and we settled down again to await nightfall.

One would imagine that in a deep valley running roughly north and south it would be difficult to decide on the actual moment of sunset, but here, knowing what to expect, this was not so. A series of dependable warnings of the approaching end of the day were delivered by birds and animals. About an hour before sunset, for example, green parakeets — which you never saw during the day — would begin to fuss and chatter like starlings in most of the tree tops. A little later the toucans would pass over dramatically. Only professional naturalists ever managed to observe these grotesque birds at close range going about their normal daily business, but a half-hour after dawn or a half-hour before sundown in the tropics the toucans would pass over, pushing their enormous beaks through the sky with a great, whistling cleavage of air. And then, as the sun set fire to the edge of the jungle, the nervous, neurotically jubilant howling of the monkeys would start, and there was never a variation of two minutes in their timing. These familiar signs of the passing of a day (and there were probably a hundred more that went unnoticed to a white man) were accepted by the Indians as being intertwined in some way, like all other natural occurrences, with the threads of human destiny. The valley had filled up with shadow, the parakeets had already gone to roost, the toucans had passed, but the monkeys had not yet been seized with their twilight hysteria, when one of the vaqueros let out an excited shout and we all looked up.

The Chilams were out on the path coming down towards us in single file, their cottons gleaming in the dusk. They were coming, rifles slung on backs, with their quick, rubbery

Indian trot. Calmo was not to be seen at first, and then I saw him come through the trotting Indians to place himself at their head. I knew something had gone wrong with the plan of operations, because although it was going to be dark in half an hour it might as well have been midday from the point of view of visibility in an attack. But just what had gone wrong? It was inconceivable that Calmo would deliberately disobey an order. 'I'll bring them in after nightfall,' he had said. Yet here he was leading them out now like targets for a battue.

It was not a question of picking out vague figures. You could see every physical detail, decide the location of a man's heart under his ribs, where his brain started above the eyebrows or, if you were a doubtful shot — or a superstition about magic shirts or the effects of poisoned alcohol were plucking at your nerves — you could aim at the large but vulnerable area roughly in the centre of the body. I ordered the men to take up firing positions, noticing that a single monkey had begun to howl, like a child singing feebly up the scale — there is always a lone howl-leader that sets the others off. At that moment the Chilams began to run, and the shooting started.

It was like a sudden summer squall that you hear on a calm day racing through the trees in a thicket some way off and then, a moment later, it is beating down the corn in the field where you stand. The Chilams were running, not very fast — rather, as Indians do, as if their legs were hobbled — when they were caught in a storm that tossed them over like flimsy scarecrows. We could see the red spurt of the rifles up in the shadowed edge of the jungle and I ordered the men to fire at the flashes and keep firing. I took my Mauser, trying to forget about the fatal weakness of Morales' breech, sighted at a point where I had seen a flash, waited till it came again, shifted the aim to allow something for the distance between the rifle's muzzle and the body of the man who held it, and pressed the trigger. The stock kicking at my shoulder jarred my teeth and the base of my skull. I worked the bolt, and fired again. I fired five times, always at the same spot, and the flashes stopped in that place. There was something about the crashing roar of my own gun that put spirit into me. I was shaking, but exultant. I took out the empty clip and pushed another home, noticing that my hand was covered in blood from the place where the trigger-guard, jolting under the gun's concussion, had cut into my thumb joint. Some figures appeared at the top of the slope. They were like motionless dummies on a fairground shooting range. I fired two rounds at them happily and they jerked out of sight. Now I lowered the rifle to look down at the road. Some of the Chilams were still to be seen moving about. They were going down to the river again, some of them dragging others, and there was space in my emotions to be surprised that Indians actually helped one another in such an emergency. My previous belief was the normal white man's conviction that they were stoical about their own fate and totally indifferent to that of others. Perhaps battle was different.

Out away from the little tangled group of struggling humanity came the short and unimposing figure of Calmo, who had now reduced speed and was strolling towards us, looking to neither side and with a touch of swagger that I found offensive. There was an occasional gun-flash in the jungle and when we saw one we all fired at the same place at once. Calmo had about thirty of his short paces to go. I could see the unnaturally calm expression on his face now, and my amazement at his blunder or his stupidity was changing to fury. I shouted to him to stop acting and get a move on. My command of the kind of Spanish you need at times like this is deficient, and I thought he smiled. At that moment he seemed to hesitate and then he raised a leg as if to go on, but rather higher than necessary as if to climb an invisible step, bringing it down in the same place. He was close enough for me to see the recognition go out of his face. He had stopped seeing the joke. Now he lifted the other leg and brought it down in the same place. He was marking time, treading air, caught in invisible quicksands. In the end he looked down at his feet as if to discover why they would no longer carry him. Then he went over sideways. We all went out together to bring him in, but he had a bullet clean through the heart. He must have died when it hit him, but in spirit he was more like a fighting-cock than a man.

I still couldn't understand how the rescue plan had so disastrously gone wrong.

18

'T̲H̲E̲ answer to the mystery is simple enough,' Helmuth Stern said. 'An Indian's day ends at sunset. The night hours don't count. Your men made a break for it when they did because their lucky day was due to come to an end in a few minutes. They probably wouldn't listen to your sergeant. What did you do with the wounded?'

'We took them to hospital.'

'You can write them off. Only a shaman can do anything for a Chilam. They only respond to sweat-baths, prayers and aguardiente. It was a waste of effort to take them to hospital. How many did you say were killed?'

'We found twelve and buried them on the spot. The vultures had started on some of them.'

'How terrible,' Lisa said. She put down her embroidery and shook her head, eyes glistening. We sat in front of the big picture window, and I fully agreed with Helmuth about it now: the view was like a tasteless painting you had lived with too long. 'The rest of them, the ones who were still on their feet, disappeared as soon as we came up. It was fairly dark by that time.'

'How many vigilantes did you get?'

'I don't know. Quite a few I hope. We didn't bother to look for them. That's Elliot's worry. I'm glad to say we managed to find the Browning, though.'

'Why?'

'Well, to put it plainly — as I see it, Elliot hired a lot of gangsters to get rid of some Indians who were in his way.'

'That's rather a dangerous allegation, isn't it?'

'The Browning's the only evidence I need, although there's plenty more.'

'I suppose it's been done so often before, when you come to think of it,' Helmuth said. 'You might as well say the whole of the American continent's been opened up in more or less the same way. Read the history of the oil companies and the rail-roads. Elliot's a babe in arms compared to some of the captains of industry of the last century. They were all highly religious. That's what made them so tough. Elliot only believes in the Life Force. You have to accept him. Elliot's evolution in a crude disguise.'

Lisa filled the glasses again. 'He looked in for a few minutes before he went off to Mexico. He was full of new schemes as usual.'

'All of which he will bring off,' Helmuth said, 'you may be quite sure of that. Oh yes, his latest idea is to teach his Indians how to have a fiesta. He's going to bring back a team of Mexican dancers so that they can all be jolly together for the Indian New Year. The New Year happens to coincide this time with the arrival of his tourists. Mind if I have some Coca-Cola in mine, darling?' He shot a glance at me and smiled apologetically.

'I think I may have a surprise in store for Elliot when he gets back,' I said. 'His gangsters happen also to have assassinated my sergeant. That, I believe, is where he made his mistake. They held a coroner's inquest this morning. I insisted on it. Needless to say, there was an open verdict which I refused to accept. Nothing could have been more obvious than that the jury had been got at. You could see it in their faces.'

'You might be able to prove murder, but from what you tell me I'm inclined to doubt it.'

'What I propose to do is to demand a Court of Inquiry into the entire Julapa business, and at the same time put the whole facts of the case before the High Command in Guatemala City. I may even get an audience with the President.'

'I'm still not sure that it'll do any good.' Helmuth shook his head. 'My advice would be to sit back and think before you do anything drastic. In these countries a fait accompli is a fait accompli, and it gets a lot of respect as such.'

'You may be right. We shall see.'

'I certainly wish you luck, David. I mean that. I think you're sticking your neck out — that's an Americanism isn't it? — I'm sorry. Anyway, it will do you good to get away from this hole.'

Lisa put down her embroidery and leaned across to us anxiously. 'I am so sorry to interrupt, but do you smell something burning?'

Helmuth dashed out of the room and we could hear him shouting. He came back and threw himself into his chair with an explosive sigh. 'It's only those fools burning the dinner again. It's a kind of traditional way they have of punishing us for existing. Do you know, I was looking through a historical manuscript the other day and I came across an account of the trial of a local woman about a hundred years ago for the murder of her cook. She had invited some friends for Sunday lunch, and the cook burned the meal for the third time in succession. The woman excused herself for a few minutes while she went away and gave orders for the cook to be tied up and thrown into the fire. After that they all went off to church. The defence asked the court to take into consideration the notorious effect of the high altitude on the temper. The woman was let off with a caution, of course. Do you know, David, I can't understand why you still worry so much — or shall I say appear to worry so much? — about the sanctity of human

167

life in a place like this. There never has been any sanctity about it, and there never will be — at least until friend Elliot has had time to get his New Order properly organized. Then perhaps you'll get justice — for the first time.'

'Tell Mr Williams about the bus,' Lisa said.

'The bus? Ah yes, well that's a splendid illustration of what I mean. A very good example indeed of the total indifference of Indians towards anyone's fate but their own. You tell David what happened.'

'We were out in the garden together trying to clear the parasites away from the apple trees,' Lisa said. 'Most people don't know — I mean even our friends from Europe didn't seem to realize that you can grow apples and pears — fruit that is worth eating and not without taste altogether, I mean — only you have to be all the time keeping the trees free of lichen and parasitic creepers — '

Helmuth jumped up and went to the window. 'If you come over here you can see where the road comes down the hill and curves round the bottom of the garden. See the gap in the wall? We'd just settled down to work when a ladino with a bus-load of Indians came full tilt down the hill — you know the way they drive?'

'And everyone was drunk,' Lisa said.

'The next thing we knew the bus smashed through the wall and came roaring down the bank into the garden. We had to jump for our lives. It cut down five of our apple trees before it overturned.'

'And do you know,' Lisa said, 'there was not a shout or a cry. Not so much as one.'

'That's absolutely right. There was the bus lying on its side, and all the passengers that could move were quietly climbing out of the windows and walking away. Mark that, they were walking away. No one was showing the slightest concern for the people still in the bus who were injured. When the driver came over and asked me for a cigarette I felt like hitting him. Our servants, by the way, came out of the house and stood there giggling.'

'I shall never understand them,' Lisa said. 'Never.'

'What I'm trying to underline,' Helmuth said, 'is that you and I have certain European standards, but they don't exist here outside ourselves, and we've got to stop being surprised and shocked whenever it is brought home to us that they don't exist. That's all. And to think that the ancestors of these people invented mathematics a thousand years before the Hindus.'

'Women who die in childbirth go straight to heaven,' Lisa said. 'And suicides. I think that's rather touching. It's the only belief they have that I approve of personally. All the rest is so heartless.'

For some reason I was reminded at that moment of the Chilam's unpicturesque New Year custom of getting ritually drunk and carrying a black box that looked like a coffin round the streets — the custom that Elliot had mentioned that he intended to suppress. 'I wonder what will become of the famous black box?' I said.

'You mean their Ark of the Covenant?' Helmuth asked. 'Heaven only knows. Probably stay wherever they've hidden it until they forget about its existence. Only a Chilam of noble origin was allowed to touch it, and they're all in the lock-up now. All the same, I'd give a good deal to know what's inside it.'

'What could there be?'

'Well, naturally, I'm being romantic, but it could be a Mayan codex, couldn't it? Most people don't rule out the possibility of one or two still existing, and it strikes me as being a likely sort of hiding-place. Think of the sensation if a new one came to light! It would be the find of the century. The idea of it makes my mouth water.'

'What do the Indians say it contains?'

'To tell you the truth, I've never thought of asking one.

Half a moment, though — ' He went to the door leading to the kitchen and shouted 'Simona!' and in a moment a small, brown-faced Indian woman appeared, with a man at her back.

'Come here,' Helmuth bawled. 'I'd almost forgotten this pair were Chilams,' he said to me. 'I expect Elliot will be wanting to take them off my hands as soon as he finds out they are here.' His voice changed. 'Well, what are you waiting for?'

'Darling,' Lisa said. 'Don't shout so. I'm sure it only makes them sillier than they would be.'

'Nonsense. It's the only way to get results.' Helmuth twisted his mild face into a semblance of ferocity, and the Indian woman moved a few inches closer, her face crumpled like a child's on the verge of tears. The man stood where he was, twisting his hands. His expression was incredibly mournful, like that of a bloodhound.

Helmuth cleared his throat. 'What's in that box of yours?' he yelped. The harsh tone of voice sounded very unnatural and strained. Most people managed to talk to Indians like this quite unconsciously in a few years, but Helmuth was still at the trying stage. It was like a nice-mannered senior boy in a school production trying to play the part of a sergeant-major.

'The box, señorito?' The Indian woman succeeded in conveying infinite incomprehension. She was about forty, but there was something about her that was terribly child-like. The Indians were like that. They wanted to remain children and they did. Later the time came when they wanted to die, and they just lay down and died. It was a sort of biological knack.

Helmuth said in Spanish, 'The black box you people carry about in your processions,' and then to me in English, 'For God's sake, look at them! They're holding their breath. Do you realize they think we poison the air,' and then, in Span-

170

ish, 'Breathe, curse you! Now come on, let's have it. What's in the box?'

The man moved up close behind the woman, eyes, jowls and shoulders sagging. 'Our god, señorito.' He was sadly apologetic to give cause for disappointment once again.

'Well, what god? You've got so many gods.'

'Zoltaca.' The woman seemed to shrivel a little, paling under her skin.

'But I thought Zoltaca was the one of the mountain tops.'

'We worship him on the mountain tops, but he is everywhere, in the sun and the sky too. Also in the box. When he is with our people he is in the box. That is the house we have made for him so that we can always have him with us.'

Helmuth looked slightly surprised, and also, I thought, deflated. 'All right, you can go,' he said. His normal voice had suddenly come back. 'Well, I suppose you can't complain about their theology. But did you notice that business of holding their breath? Most people think they admire us, but don't you believe it. Do you know what they call us in Chilam? — ghosts. I used to think it funny. It used to make me laugh when I heard them say "have you taken the ghosts their coffee?" or "the female ghost has one of her headaches this afternoon". I never let them know that I understood Chilam. Now I don't see the joke any more. They really mean it, and it makes me shiver.'

I looked at my watch. 'I'm afraid I shall have to be making a move,' I said. 'The plane takes off in just over an hour.'

'Oh yes, of course. How silly of us to keep you. And look here, don't bother about the parcel for the museum this time. When I mentioned it I'm afraid I didn't realize how things had turned out. You'll have enough to bother you without running errands.'

'That will be all right,' I told him. 'There won't be any trouble at all. I know only too well the amount of time I'll probably have on my hands. I'll be very pleased to do it.'

'And when shall we be seeing you again, Mr Williams?' Lisa asked.

'That I'm afraid I can't say. As you know, I've not a great wish to come back here. If I can avoid coming back I shall. If not — well — I hope we'll meet again soon, in Guatemala City perhaps.'

I went out and got into Elliot's jeep, crashed the gears and took off with rear wheels spinning. Helmuth and Lisa stood on the top of the hill and waved until I passed the gap in their garden wall, and then I turned the corner so that the house was out of sight. I really did not think I should see them again, because I wanted to make some very definite move. A move that would bring my stay in Guadaloupe to an immediate end.

19

F ROM the moment the plane touched down at Aurora
Airfield, Guatemala City, I felt my confidence begin to
wane. This was another world. The very air one breathed
was different. Guadaloupe seemed very far away, and it was
a long time indeed since the battle in the ravine at Julapa.

I found the City much changed. It was as beautiful and
indifferent as the angel-faced women who paraded its aven-
ues in physical preparation for the evening meal. It had put
on Cadillacs and soda-fountains like fat round the waist.
On the surface life had fallen into the smooth rhythms of
afternoon-tea music played by a ladies' string quartette.
Newly imported goods glittered in the shop windows; the
cinemas offered the latest super-productions; traffic-lights
winked impartially at Buicks and ox-carts; American business executives stood up in the best bars and called for their
drinks in policy-decision voices. A banner stretched across
Sixth Avenue that startled me for a moment with the single
word SACRIFICE turned out to refer to a sale of aluminium
kitchenware. It was hard to believe that tanks could have
rumbled up and down these sleek streets a few weeks before,
and also on many other occasions in the last twenty years.
So far as it was found necessary — as I later discovered — to
eliminate opponents of the régime, it was now done without
any fuss or publicity at the police station, which looks like a
Moorish palace.

At Army H.Q. they seemed surprised when I asked for Kranz. I learned that he had to be approached through an intermediary, one Major Somoza. I sat down unimportantly in the anteroom of Somoza's office with a great number of others who were coming to grips with the realization of their own insignificance. The city was winning its war of nerves with me. The urgency of my small affairs dwindled constantly in the face of the smooth indifference of the military bureaucracy. I realized that yet another new picture of Balboa was on display. He had been photographed from a low angle that turned him into a handsome, contemptuous man with a big jaw. I observed also that he had taken to the use of the kind of high-crowned military hat once favoured by the leading lights in Nazi Germany. The door opened, releasing gusts of vigorous laughter, and I caught a glimpse of the major at his desk. It was the regular officer who had ordered the massacre I had witnessed in the jungle on the day the revolution had ended.

I got up and went out quickly. I picked up a taxi outside the building and told the driver to take me to the Parque Central. Here I sat on a bench under the trees and watched a war-mutilated beggar playing his flute and the spindly Indians of Guatemala City going by with wardrobes and settees on their backs, and thought about things. After a while I remembered that Kranz had once spoken of the San Carlos as his favourite hotel, and had said that he was going to move in there as soon as they could find a room for him. I walked over and found him there.

Kranz was installed in an elaborate suite with satin bed coverlets and good aquatints on the wall, and I detected from the first moment a quite unmistakable ozone of feminine occupation. He had put on at least fifteen pounds since I last saw him and there was a creaminess about his skin that was probably the result of a well-planned diet. He came at me with both hands outstretched, but there was a blankness of expression that made me doubt for a moment if he remembered who I was.

'Mais, qu'est-ce que tu fais ici?' He recognized me now, but he hadn't the faintest idea where I'd been. Oceans of time and chance separated him from the evening when we had last seen each other a few weeks before.

'Well, in the first place,' I told him, 'I want to hand in my resignation. Whom do I have to see?'

Kranz let go my imprisoned hand and picked up the telephone. 'What can I offer you to drink?'

'Anything,' I said. 'Make it a whisky-soda.'

'Two highballs,' Kranz said into the phone severely. 'With Scotch — not, if you please, with Bourbon, as last time.' He turned to me. 'You are utterly and completely crazy, of course. You are being paid a lot of money to carry a pistol and make faces at people. I personally know many people who could use a job like that.'

'Fine. I'm glad to hear it. Anyway, that's the first purpose of my visit. Secondly, I'd like to know what the chances are of an audience with the President.'

'Your finca, isn't it? I guess the President's time is pretty well taken up these days.'

'No. It doesn't happen to be the finca. I've produced a report, and I want to see that it gets into his hands.'

'Have you got it? Show it to me.'

I opened my dispatch-case and took out the sheaf of papers. Kranz accepted them gingerly. He managed to look as if he were bothered by an extremely small fly which had just blown into his eye. He made a pretence of scanning the top sheet, pursed his lips and nodded a few times. 'I should like you to leave this with me for a few hours. You can spare it?' It was like a theatrical producer offering to read a beginner's play. I couldn't help laughing.

Kranz looked slightly hurt, but the situation was eased by the arrival of the drinks. He picked up the now familiar bottle with the kilted Highlander on the label, sniffed it and shook his head, manufacturing a little false indignation. 'Ah, ces gens! Anyhow, it will be better than their Bourbon.'

We clinked glasses and Kranz patted me on the shoulder affectionately. 'And how is life in Palín?'

'Guadaloupe,' I told him, hope draining away steadily.

'Of course. Yes. Why do I always say Palín? I mean Guadaloupe. That's a nice place. I tell you, you are lucky. Here, for example, it is nothing. What is it? A town with some big hotels that are full up with business conventions all the time. You might as well be in Buffalo.'

'I half expected you'd be Minister for War by now. Done anything about taking out citizenship papers?'

Kranz picked up a polished copper model of a sailing ship, stared at it with gloomy distaste for a moment, and turned on me. 'Do you know what they have done, David? They have made me into a policeman.' He sniffed like a child in need of comfort. 'I am an old warhorse. I long for the scent of burnt powder in my nostrils. And what do I become? A one-man Gestapo.'

'That's what comes of being German,' I said. 'It's the national reputation.'

'There are always silly boys who do not think their advancement in the army or in politics is fast enough, so they make plots. These plots they unfailingly reveal to the beautiful girls they take to bed, because here it is very important to make a plot. After that, of course, the beautiful girl confides the story to another of the young men who implore her to sleep with them, because if one cannot make a plot it is at least something to know about one. Then we must go in the night for the first silly boy, and endure the terrible scene when we take him from his mother and bring him to a place where they will invite him to drink half a bottle of brandy before shooting him in the neck.'

'The German method again.'

'You think that Germans have a special aptitude for these things. I assure you I have never witnessed the final ceremony. This is not for me.'

'Putting aside the unpleasant details, I should still have said you'd done pretty well for yourself.'

Kranz shook his head and his massive cheeks vibrated. 'I crave movement, adventure, the unforeseen. I do not wish to be involved in State receptions, cocktail parties for the American Vice-President, the hypocrisy of solemn masses in the Cathedral for the souls of those we have killed, or the assassination by night of silly, young, weeping boys. These things are stifling me. I am by nature a nomad.' He belched quietly and patted his thickened midriff. 'I am like a caged lion.'

'In that case, I hope you can sympathize with me, or at least that you will after you've read that report.'

'Yes, yes, of course I sympathize with you. But I think our cases are a little different, are they not? You are by nature a settled man; one who has been uprooted. Soon you will get your finca back. The dates have already been published in the papers. After that everything will be good for you. I do not think it is too late for you to marry and to have three or four children, whom you will send to your country, where nothing changes, to receive their proper education. These things do not apply to a man without a country, especially to one who has a little of the gypsy in his blood. I hope I will witness your happiness.'

'I don't think you ever will. Not that kind of happiness. Besides which, I'm not fool enough to think I'll get the finca back unless I go on doing what I'm told — ' I stopped because Kranz wasn't listening. The noise of someone moving things about in the next room had become more insistent in the last few minutes and now I heard a feminine cough, musical but emphatic. I felt that Kranz wanted me to go, so I got up.

'Off already, David? You've only just arrived. Well, in that case we must get together again soon, eh?'

'The report — ' I reminded him. 'You were going to run over it.'

'Why yes, of course I was. Well here's a better idea. You are doing something tonight? No? That's fine. Then let's go somewhere and relax and talk things over. In the meanwhile I'll try to find time to go through your report. Make it after dinner, shall we? About ten o'clock suit you?'

'All right then. I'll pick you up.'

'Fine. We'll go to a quiet place where we can relax. Maybe a little music — eh?' He hesitated. 'You don't object if I happen to have a friend with me?'

'Not in the slightest.'

'If you have a friend, bring her along too, of course. That would be better still.'

'I haven't at the moment,' I told him.

———————

20

Kranz's friend turned out to be a splendid wide-eyed mulatta from Livingstone on the Atlantic coast, where there is a mainly black colony. She was swathed in crooner's gold lamé and moved to a tiny tinkling orchestra of bizarre ornaments and with a gentle undulation of the torso, as if in the arms of an invisible dancing partner. Movie-English is the language down in Livingstone, and Aneta called us both Baby. We took a car over to El Gallito, and when she left us for a moment Kranz looked about him nervously, and then said in a hoarse whisper: 'She has a lick of the tar-brush.' He looked at me with a kind of anxiety and added: 'That poor little girl's had a raw deal all round.'

The poor little girl came back in a shimmer of gold. She held herself like somebody at the head of a procession. When anyone turned to look at her Aneta would smile widely at them. I was beginning to take in the details. Her eyes were so big that there hardly seemed enough room for the other features, and she wore ivory ear-rings like bangles. I have often noticed that questing men like Kranz develop a taste for extreme exoticism in their women, in the way a Southern planter is driven to flail his palate with more and more tabasco sauce.

Aneta was familiar with the waiters and she knew the marimba players by name. They all benefited from the same wide, encouraging smile. I suspected that she had worked in places like this. When she and Kranz danced together, Kranz's natural dignity, which was considerable — as is often the case in that kind of heavy-bodied, slow-moving man — fell away from him, and he shambled after her like a performing bear with memories of the burning iron at the back of its brain. Kranz had taken off his coat, and his shirt was wet between the shoulder-blades and round the arm-pits. He traipsed stolidly forward, face gone imbecile, while Aneta tapped with mother-of-pearl enamelled nails on the red skin of his neck and swept the room over his shoulder with her inviting gaze. The sad-faced men who played the giant marimba — twelve of them — had galloped off into a *son* — a furious, drunken Indian version of the paso-doble — and every so often Kranz missed a beat, stumbled, and Aneta caught and steadied him without a flicker of concern. There was a wonderful arrangement of steel muscles under the coffee-coloured silk of her skin. The band stopped with a final, nerve-cracking crash of hammers, and they came back. Kranz slumped in his chair, red-rimmed eyes afloat in sweat. He fussed quickly to cover the bare patch of scalp that had appeared over his left ear. The marimba players picked up their hammers and struck an opening chord and Aneta held out a beautiful bronze arm towards me, but I smiled and shook my head, and before Kranz could muster his resistance a bowing, swarthy young man appeared and carried her away.

Kranz followed her with deprived eyes as she melted into the human whirlpool on the floor. He ordered a double whisky-on-the-rocks in a groaning voice. I stayed with my highball. Kranz, I thought, was slightly stewed already. He stopped looking unhappily at the dancing couples. 'I've read your report, my boy. Forgive me, but I still think you are crazy. Je ne te comprends pas. Also I think you are making mountains out of molehills.'

'Well, I don't think so.'

'You are too close to things to view them in proper perspective. Palín is a small town. It is also rather a long way away. The President is very busy, I assure you. Very busy indeed. You can't be expected to see the kind of things that are happening here all the time when you are in Palín.'

'Guadaloupe,' I said.

'I am sorry — Guadaloupe.'

'You had time to go right through the report?' I asked him. My suspicions were growing.

'I made time. And there again, the basis of the complaint you raise isn't entirely trivial. At any other time interference with water supplies is a serious business — but you have to understand, my boy, that seen in relation to the big problems of the moment — well — it loses some importance. I'm being frank.'

'Interference with water supplies — ?' I began. 'What on earth — ?'

Kranz wasn't listening. 'Come back in a month's time, and you'll get action. The dam will be dismantled — if necessary, blown up. I sit back and I see the whole plan in operation. Perhaps both of us are deprived of proper perspective. You are short-sighted. My sight is defective in the other sense.'

I saw it was hopeless to talk to him. He was very tired and slightly drunk, and at that moment perhaps a little past it. We saw Aneta and her partner break out of the crowd and come towards us. It was like the performance of a pair of cabaret artists; tremendously smooth and complicated and nonchalant. The man, who possessed a long, supercilious nose, and hair brushed like a duck's plumage into the nape of his neck, had his left hand resting just above Aneta's hip. Aneta's smile came and went like a beacon. She pirouetted away from her partner, took a drink out of Kranz's glass, and went back with a snap of fingers and heels to the waiting arms. 'Untermenschen,' Kranz said. 'It is a German word I don't know how to say in English. It means inferior, but more than that. I refer to the males. You can say I am superstitious. I still believe that there are inferior peoples. This people is inferior. They are all puppy-dogs and mothers' boys. The men, I mean. How old are you, David?'

'Thirty-eight.'

'Then you are a man of the 'thirties?'

'I don't follow you.'

'I mean that you are a product of the days when it was good to be alive. Do you remember what it was like — the tension, the precarious existence, the sense of purpose, of destiny?'

'I know what you mean all right — even if I didn't find it so enjoyable as you probably did.'

Kranz shook his head. 'I was S.S. One of the first. I mean the selected ones before they let anyone come in who liked to ask. But now it's all over. All the wonderful wars are over, David. There won't be any more. Do you realize that?'

'That's a matter of opinion. It certainly isn't mine.'

'They're over David, make no mistake. No Adolf to keep us on our toes now. Have you been in Europe lately? I have. I spent two years there. It's gone soft. It's silly. A life for an old man. Do you know what I like about Central America? You're back in the 'thirties again. You have to worry a little about keeping alive. Not very much. But just enough. The right amount. I've got to say this for Guatemala. It's given me back my youth again. Here I am a young man.' Kranz had wiped the sweat out of his eyes, but they seemed to water again at a recollection.

'I should have said that Balboa was a pretty poor substitute for Adolf.'

Kranz sighed. 'And he has no cause, that is the trouble.

Adolf always had a cause. Here a cause is used up very quickly — in a week or two at the most. After that it maybe takes them years to find another cause.' I saw the hungry look come into his eyes again and I knew without following them that Aneta was in sight. 'I'd have made a move long before now,' Kranz said. 'Do you know what kept me back? The thought of having to go away and leave that little girl. She's terribly dependent upon me.'

Aneta came and settled on her chair with the grace of a beautiful bird. She sipped her soft drink and asked for some nuts. When the nuts came she put several on the tip of a bluish tongue, and Kranz watched fondly while she withdrew them from sight and began to munch. 'Don't look so worried, baby,' she said to me. 'Why do you look so worried all the time?'

'Because that's the way I feel, I suppose — if that's a good enough reason.'

'Aw, he doesn't have to feel worried, does he, baby? You don't have to feel worried.'

Kranz never bothered to talk to her. He was one of those lovers who find conversation unnecessary. He also had a habit of talking to me in front of her as if she wasn't there. 'She has a marked feeling of insecurity,' he said. 'Naturally, that's to be expected.' The marimba players' hammers crashed down. I saw the young man with the horse face making for our table, and the uneasy look came into Kranz's eyes. He nodded to me and I took Aneta on to the floor.

'You one of his bunch — flat-foot, I mean?'

'Well no, not really.'

'Army officer, then?'

'Mm. Temporarily.'

'Do you know I kinda thought you was. Going to stick around a bit?'

'Not any longer than I can help.'

The slow, thick speech still came as a surprise. It did not

183

go with anything about her. She had electricity, as they say in Latin-America. *Electricidad*. When I touched her skin I imagined that my finger-tips tingled. And she had a power of communicating rhythm that was a new experience to me. I gave up trying to lead and left it to her and we swung and whirled like dervishes. Then the floor filled up and we were trapped tight in a corner again face to face.

'You like me?'

'I think you dance very well.'

'I din ask you that. That's not what I asked you.'

'All right, then I like you,' — which was true enough in a way, although I could have added that she startled me as well.

'You doan act like you do. When a guy likes me he usually acts like he does.' I wondered at the deformed speech in that perfect mouth.

'Say, you listening?'

'And how does a guy act?'

'Well, Jeeze, he takes proper hold of me for one thing. For crissakes, I got a case of body odour or something? Well, that's better. That's a *lot* better. Say listen, David — that's your name ain't it — why doan you stick around a bit? Maybe you and me could see something of each other some time.

'What about Kranz?'

'Thinkin' of your old pal, eh? Well, you can forget about him. He's pulling out. Din he tell you that? He din tell me either, but I know all the same. I guess he's all washed up here. Do you want to know something? He's buying me a candy store on Sixth Avenue to break the blow. It's going to be a lovely surprise.' She made a face — a very ugly face, as a pretty woman sometimes can.

'Well, you can always sell it.'

'No, I can't. He thought of that one. It's all fixed up somehow so it can't be sold. Doan ask me how, but that's how it is.'

184

The pack-ice on the floor broke up suddenly as the music stopped, and we went back to Kranz.

Aneta excused herself and Kranz turned a reddened eye on me. He seemed suddenly to have lost his shape, as if the heat had softened his bones.

'Did she ask you to take her on?'

'Did she what?' I felt my colour change and I swallowed my saliva. I was furious to realize that I was behaving as if I had been caught in a guilty intrigue.

'I think that we are safe to say that she did. I was wondering if she would do that.' He suddenly groped forward towards me and put two solicitous hands on my shoulders. 'Don't think for a moment I'm reproaching you, my dear boy. Nor am I blaming the girl — pauvre enfant.'

'She said she wouldn't mind seeing me again. I don't know if there's anything extraordinary about that.'

'Of course there's nothing extraordinary about it, but it tells me that she's found out. That's all.'

'I told her, by the way, that my time was pretty fully taken up.' Actually that was what I should have told her if the music hadn't stopped when it did.

Kranz released my shoulders. He burped like a baby. 'I wouldn't have blamed you in the least, David. You're a gentleman, you're an honourable man, and you're my friend. I talk like this because — as you see — I've had quite a number of drinks. I've a surprise for you, David ... Should have let you into the secret earlier. I'm moving on. It's going to be hard. Aneta's got a great sense of loyalty to me but she feels very insecure. I wouldn't feel quite so bad in here' — he dug into his solar plexus with his fist — 'if I thought that there was someone like you to take care of her. She's above this rotten crowd, David.'

Wishing to pass over the matter of Aneta, I waited.

'What did you say?' Kranz swivelled stiffly. 'Would you mind to come and sit on the other side of me? It's my left ear. People sometimes think I'm deaf. But it's these airless places. I get a kind of buzzing in the ear. I was going to tell you something, wasn't I?'

'You said you were going away.'

'Yes, I know, but there was something else. Ah yes, your coffee finca. That was it. You're getting it back. Well? Don't you feel happy? You want to sing or something?'

'Of course I do. Naturally.' In reality I felt nothing in particular, except some surprise that I should have been able to take the news so coolly.

'I checked up after you left this morning. It's a matter of days or weeks at most. It's gone through, that's the main thing. Is that her coming?'

'No,' I told him. It was another coloured girl in gold lamé, but very unlike Aneta. I gathered that Kranz, who never wore spectacles, couldn't tell one face from another at ten yards.

'If I were you, what I would do would be to go away quietly and sit down and wait. I would take great care not to make a nuisance of myself. Faut pas emmerder les gens. She is taking her time, isn't she? Would you give me a straight answer to a straight question?'

'Probably.'

'It is very difficult for me to ask you this — but do you feel like taking her over?'

'No.'

'That is final? I mean there is no chance you will change your mind?'

'None at all.'

'That is a pity, because she has many things to recommend her,' Kranz said miserably, 'and I think that security would transform her. A beautiful girl like that. I have a little thing about a business all fixed up, but I don't know. You'll be settling down now. She needs a guiding hand.'

'I've had all the trouble I want for a while. Why don't you stay if you're worried? Or take her with you?'

'I can't explain it, David. Put it down to destiny, if you like. I feel my destiny driving me on, and whatever I must face, I must face alone.'

When Kranz said destiny he meant vanity. Vanity drove him cruelly. He always wanted, above all things, to go on thinking of himself as a boyish adventurer.

'Where are you off to this time then?'

Kranz brightened. 'I have been offered something very interesting. A straightforward job of reorganizing. I'm reorganizing an army. No more Banana Republics. No more nonsense with jungles and Indians. It's something very big. The kind of thing you dream about.'

'When do you start work?'

Kranz dropped his voice. 'There are a few preliminaries to be attended to. It may be a month or two, but I'm flying down there in a few days to be on the spot. The present staff has to be got rid of.'

'And they're likely to object? That's it, isn't it?'

'They may. I don't say they won't. But then we always have the Air Force to fall back on. Maybe the Navy too. We're not pinning too much faith on the Navy.'

I was beginning to see daylight. 'Didn't you say that this was a straightforward job of reorganizing?'

'Yes, certainly — after the coup d'état has succeeded. We expect the present government to fall very shortly. After that I reorganize. Would you like a job? I could probably find one for you.'

'Do you mean that seriously?'

'Of course I do. I would like to have you with me.'

'It all sounds a bit too fantastic for my liking.'

'Does it?' Kranz was really surprised.

'When the revolution comes off you are going to reorganize the army. If the revolution comes off. And if the new government doesn't change its mind, as they so often do. Well, I mean, doesn't it all sound a bit chancy to you?'

Kranz looked at me with a kind of compassion. 'Forgive me — I forgot all about the finca. You are a man of property now, David. I think you are in a hurry to get back to that farm. I think, too, that there is nothing like coming into possessions to bring about a quick change in the outlook.'

I felt a slight resentment at this suggestion that any criticism of Kranz's absurd adventures must necessarily mean that I was turning into an unimaginative bourgeois. I was about to defend myself when I saw a familiar glitter at the back of the crowd. 'Your girl's coming,' I told him.

'Ah,' he said. The excitement left him and he was sad and deflated again. 'So she is. Well anyway, David — bear it in mind. There's a job for the taking. Maybe the finca could wait for a few months. I'd like to have someone I can depend upon with me.'

21

I WENT to bed and lay awake listening to the heavy silk of traffic rustling in the streets, and the soft, distant brass of car horns. I was trying to decide on my next move, and my thoughts were pushing sleep farther and farther away. First of all the finca. It was within my grasp now, and it looked as though all I had to do was to keep quiet and not make a nuisance of myself. I was unhappy about my inability to feel excited about the prospect of once more becoming a land-owner. For five years I had gone on day-dreaming of myself fitted back neatly into the jigsaw of bourgeois exist- ence. I would reclaim the finca and equip myself with one of those model Latin-American wives of which there was always a fair choice at the disposition of finca-owners — women of tough fibre beneath their shell of femininity; precise and predictable within their limitations. She would bring time and order and routine into my life and do me honour before my fellows. She would exorcize all that Greta had stood for; the brief raptures, the dishonour, the sterility and the drift. I couldn't imagine restarting my life at the finca with Greta by my side. But neither at this time could I feel any en- thusiasm for the conventional alternative and all that went with it in the way of slow accumulations, hard-won recogni- tions and slight triumphs.

The purpose of my visit to the city occupied the next two days, but I found myself getting nowhere. I could find no way of reaching the ear of any of the President's secretaries. Time was running out. Causes, like everything else in that climate, stale rapidly.

I remembered that Don Arturo had been interested in some humanitarian cause, although I couldn't recollect what it was, and I went to see the old man. When I inquired about this activity of his it produced a little flare-up of enthusiasm.

'Why, absolutely, dear boy. I was the founder of the local branch of Our Dumb Friends' League.' He became sadly philosophical. 'Can't say really, though, that we ever made much — ah — headway. Always treated their poor animals damnably here, and still do. Had a jolly good membership, too, at one time. That was quite a while ago. And in the end — you know what it is — ' under the sudden pressure of emotion the old man slipped unconsciously into Spanish — '*es que se murieron casi todos*.' He recovered with a start and tried to put this harshly direct Spanish reference to death into proper English. 'The fact is they've nearly all — ah — passed on now.'

A lean cat winding through a forest of bamboo chair legs paused to spray my ankle with a stinking discharge. I brought up the topic of Indians in general and saw the interest drain out of Don Arturo's face. 'The truth is, dear boy, I've never really given them much thought. Get used to seeing them about the place. Always with us — ah— like the poor. Suppose that's what it is. Do let me pour you some more tea.'

It was quite clear that the Indians hadn't any hope of competing with Our Dumb Friends for the little store of compassion that old Don Arturo had left to dispense.

When I thought of Hernandez it was as a last resort, and the more thought I gave to the possibility of throwing the whole thing into the lap of the Press, the more dangerous it sounded. A nation-wide scandal might well put a spoke in Elliot's wheel, but it would almost certainly put an end to any prospects I might have in the country — even if the military authorities didn't come down on me for giving away official secrets. After several hours' struggle with my conscience I went over to the *Noticias* office, and Hernandez saw me straight away.

Meeting him again I realized what a good fellow he was. I had always liked Hernandez, I decided. He was a good-hearted, affectionate sort of chap. A simple man. As nice a fellow as you could hope to find in this part of the world. We hugged each other in the local manner. I could see that Hernandez was genuinely pleased to see me again — just as pleased as I was to see him. 'What's new, amigo?' I asked, clapping him on the back a few more times.

'What's new? Well, I don't know.' He nodded at the lettering on the glass door. 'You see they've made me an assistant editor. That's why I'm still here at this time of the day. I don't have any time to lead my own life any more.'

'How about the movies?' I asked him.

'The movies? I haven't seen one for a week. We have Cinemascope now.'

'How do you like it?'

'Wonderful. How about taking in a show tonight? If you can hang on for an hour I'll be clear here.'

'I can't,' I told him. 'I'd have liked to, but I've got something rather important on. And, by the way, I wonder if you can spare a moment to look at this. I think you'll find it interesting.' I handed him the report. 'If you want to do anything about it,' I said, 'it'll have to be handled discreetly, and you'll have to find some way of keeping my name out, or I'll find myself in a military clink.'

'Don't give it a thought.' Hernandez gave me a knowing wink. 'It's all part of the job.' He started to read and in less than a minute he looked up. 'Why, this is terrible! It's shocking — unbelievable. I'd never have credited it. If you don't mind, David, I'm going to get down the facts and then you can have this back.' He put a sheet of paper in a typewriter and began to type. After another minute or so he looked up at me again and shook his head. 'You know, it's quite incredible the things that can go on and nobody ever gets to hear about them.'

'You think something can be done, then, about publishing the facts?'

'Think something can be done? Why this is sensational. You know, half our trouble is we're complacent. We have to be shaken right out of our complacency every so often. This is going to be a regular sensation.'

'Good,' I said. 'That's just what I want.'

When I left, Hernandez was still rolling his head in horror. He came to the street door with me to shake hands again. 'Just wait till you see our front page tomorrow morning.'

Next morning I bought a copy of *Noticias* but there was nothing to interest me on any of the pages. I rang Hernandez. 'Hullo, Hernandez. What happened to the story?'

'It was crowded out at the last moment. We had a crisis.'

'You mean you ran into some opposition from up top?' I had been half expecting that.

'Opposition? No — of course not. The editor thought the story was fine — but didn't you see what happened last night?'

'No. What happened?'

'Deborah Roberts arrived on a flying visit. You know — the film star. We got a scoop interview, but it meant resetting half the paper.'

'I see. Of course — that would explain it.'

'It's disappointing,' Hernandez said, and I could tell by his tone that he was genuinely upset, 'but it's the way things are in this game. It meant holding the story over at the last minute.'

'Holding it over?' I said hopefully.

'Well, we don't come out tomorrow, and Monday's more or less a sports sheet with all the week-end games to cover.'

'Ah.'

'We'd have liked to run it on Monday, if there'd been more space to play with. After that there's the topical angle to worry about. Anyway, David, we're going to do all we can. You know how I feel about it.'

'Of course I do. And thanks very much all the same.' So that was that. I could see now that I was wasting my time.

After that, I wrote to Army Headquarters with a formal request for my discharge, and I sent a telegram to the overseer at the finca, telling him I would be coming. Next morning I took the Guadaloupe train and got off at Coima, which we rattled into two hours late in the early afternoon. At Coima I boarded the bus which stands waiting under the tree-cactus marking the whistle-stop, and went up to Istapa.

As the crow flies, Istapa is not far from Guadaloupe, but it is on the other side of the mountains. This village, confidently marked on the national map, consists of one building: a small general store which is slowly rotting away in the fairly dry climate. I stopped to say buenos dias to the storekeeper, Don Armando, and to borrow a mule from him. I found him as I had left him five years before, lying on his bed, his goods piled around him, groaning with malaria. It was two miles uphill from Istapa through wonderful coffee country, and I was surprised to see that several of the family plantations looked in good shape. I was waiting for the excitement that I was quite sure the sight of the old, familiar scenes would bring, but it did not come. It did not even come at the first sight of our house with its untypical Californian-mission façade built by my grandfather, a Welsh romantic.

Ignacio, the overseer, was waiting at the door, hat held

like a shield over his heart. He had shrunk a little in the five years. That was all. Ignacio was the ladino version of the old family negro retainer idealized by film makers— even to the white hair; although he probably had a little more quiet malice than the negro original.

I went in, and my childhood was there again, perfectly embalmed in the odour of scented woods, brought to life even by the changeless squeak of the door. For a moment I was choked by nostalgia. Unable to speak, I held Ignacio's hands and we grinned at each other foolishly, and when I let go his hands he wiped his eyes. I noticed that as a sign of respect he was wearing no shoes.

Maria, Ignacio's old wife, came in beaming with delight, with the tea tray. I sipped the tea, catching the flavour of the goat's milk I had always detested, and nibbled at a maize cake with pretended enjoyment. Nothing about the place had changed. Nothing had been touched. My father, who had less energy but more taste than my grandfather, had completed this house, building its interior of rare and beautiful woods from the forest of El Petén, and I could never forget the honeyed, resinous scent that came from the walls. The bareness of the house was responsible for a strange acoustic quality, and as soon as I spoke and noticed my voice booming a little, I had a picture of my grandfather baying his magnificent, empty Welsh eloquence as he sat here in the last days of his life.

Ignacio had a great deal to tell me. There was a kind of sly pride in his manner. He had made a religion of his service to our family, and I knew he would have defended our interests when the need arose with every trick and subterfuge and cunning manœuvre he could think of. Maria collected the tray and dismissed herself. Ignacio ostentatiously ensured that there was no one listening at the door or the window before he began his tale.

'For the first month after you left you might say that nothing happened. We just carried on. Then one day the government instructor turned up and lectured the peones on their rights. Naturally I kept my opinions to myself. I pretended to go along with him. A few days later two caporales came to the house. Sanchez — do you remember him? — and another one who's left since.'

(Sanchez? I remembered Sanchez all right. Sanchez was one of those strange freaks, a semi-literate Indian. He was a sullen, proud young man, but also a hard worker who kept off the drink, so my father made him a caporal, which is a sort of foreman).

'Sanchez did all the talking. "Don't think we've got anything against you personally, patron, but as you probably realize the land has reverted to us now." He actually pulled out a copy of the government edict and read it out to me. I had to help him with one or two passages.

' "Come in, gentlemen," I said, "and allow me to relieve you of your hats. I'm here to assist you. Consider me at your service at all times. Now what is there you would like me to do?" Naturally, I couldn't tell you about all this in the letters, sir.' (Ignacio had been in the habit, whenever I had a postal address, of sending me monthly reports, very short and of necessity unrevealing, enclosed in yellowed, parchment envelopes from my father's escritoire, which with their heavy seals always looked like State documents.)

' "We want to grow maize and beans," Sanchez says. He pulls out another piece of paper and reads from it. "The ancestors of the Indian people lived and developed their great civilization on a diet of maize and beans. These are their only basic necessities."

' "Isn't it a fact," I said — becoming for the purposes of the argument an Indian myself — "that we also get down a fair amount of aguardiente?"

' "In the future," Sanchez says, "we will do without alcohol. Alcohol debases the people's morale and defeats their purpose." These were his actual words. I can hear him now. I thought, what's going to happen to us as employers of labour if they really give up aguardiente? "What are your plans?" I asked them.

' "First of all," Sanchez says, "we propose to cut down the coffee trees."

' "All the trees?" I ask. I may as well say that I knew that this was already happening on the other plantations. I was racking my brains to think of some way of saving the trees, but I knew that one word out of place and Sanchez would have killed me.

'Sanchez says: "We're cutting down all the trees, and after that we're planting maize and beans. Perhaps a little squash. The instructor said that that was necessary to have a properly balanced diet."

' "The coffee crop will be ready in three weeks," I say. "You don't want to collect it? After all, nine-tenths of the work is done."

' "What's the use?" Sanchez says. "The Indian people do not want coffee. Neither do they need to sell it. We need nothing from the outside world." '

'I suppose that's perfectly true, too,' I said.

'Well, sir, that's what I thought, too, while Sanchez and his friend were sitting there with their machetes on their knees. They didn't want anything, either, I thought. I was trying to think of some way to save the trees. "Well," I said, "you gentlemen have evidently taken your decision. You must do what you think best. If I can be of any assistance of course — "

'My impression is that they came expecting trouble from me, but when they saw I was quite calm and reasonable about it all they calmed down. "I want to say on behalf of the plantation workers," Sanchez says, "that there's nothing against you personally, except as a representative of the old order. If you want to join us you're at liberty to do so.

You'll do your share of the work and get your share of the crop like anyone else. Private ownership's abolished."

' "Is that a government order, too?" I asked him.

' "No. That's the will of the Indian people," he tells me.

' "Very well," I said. "That's understood. By the way, how long do you think it'll take us to grow a crop of maize and beans?"

' "If the weather's kind to us, three months."

' "And what are we going to live on until then?"

' "We'll live on our fat. The Indians ask for little. We'll get through somehow."

'I had an idea. "You've got fifteen thousand coffee trees to cut down before you can start sowing. That'll take a month."

' "We could do the clearing a bit at a time," Sanchez says. I was beginning to feel hope for the first time.

' "Why not start with the new plantation, and get that under seed first. That's the way I'd set about it," I told them. "Besides that, you've got convenient irrigation from the well under the hill. It would be easy to irrigate that land and get the crops up quick."

'And so,' Ignacio said, 'they cut down the new plantation.' His expression was that of a man tasting bitter medicine. 'We lost three years of our labour in three days' work with the axe. But what was there to be done? After that they planted their maize and their beans.' His face changed suddenly. 'It couldn't have been a week before Sanchez turned up at the house again. "My little daughter has been bitten by a snake," he says — you know, they've got to look on me as a kind of doctor and midwife combined here. "Well where is she?" I said. "Didn't you bring her?"

' "She's dead," he says. I might have known as much by the silly sort of half-grin he had on his face.

' "What do you want then?" I asked him.

' "A coffin," he says.

' "What's to stop you making one?"

' "There's no proper wood left," he says. He meant iron-wood. They've got into the habit of using ironwood, and now they won't use anything else. Here's the answer to our problem, I thought. "I've got a box here that might do," I told him. He looked at it. "No," he says, "the worms would get at her. The worms would eat her." '

(I remembered now this peculiarity of our peones, who were mostly Mams. Unlike the Chilams they had always been under the Spanish heel, and the little Christianity they absorbed was entirely a matter of dogma. They believed in the resurrection of the dead, and it was the thing they bothered most about. The completely un-Christianized Chilams were very spiritual in their beliefs. The body was absolutely of no importance. They buried their dead, when they were allowed to do so, under the floors of their huts, where the spirit could always be conveniently included in the family conversation. The Chilams did not see death at all as we saw it, and our lack of information on the subject of the hereafter was one of the things that caused them to be so un-receptive to missionary efforts. Not that anyone cared much in these days about saving the souls of Indians.)

'I told him Don Armando would supply an ironwood coffin for fifty quetzals,' Ignacio said. His tone made me look up. At this moment he didn't look so much like a gentle old whisky advertisement retainer as a picture by an old master of a Florentine banker.

'How could he ever hope to lay hands on fifty quetzals'? Ignacio smiled thinly. 'There wasn't that amount of money in the whole finca. As you know, señorito, the peones are always in debt for at least a year after a funeral. "What am I going to do, patron?" he asks. "I can't put my girl in the earth without a real coffin. I'd walk all the way to El Petén and bring the wood, but the worms would start before I got back."

' "Sell some coffee," I told him. "There's your answer. Don Armando will buy the crop on the tree."

'Well, he went away and talked it over with the rest of them and then he came back and said they had agreed to sell enough coffee for him to buy a coffin. We fetched Don Armando and they worked out the price of the coffee between them to the kilogram. They haggled over it like Jews. They let him take away just enough to cover the price of the coffin and a mass for the child's soul and not a centavo's worth more. The rest was to be left to rot on the trees. And then do you know, just at that moment, Almighty God saw fit to come to our aid. He sent a measles epidemic and it carried off half the children. They had to collect all the rest of the coffee to pay for the coffins.

'From that time on it was smooth sailing. Next year, when the time came, I told them that no one could say when God might see fit to visit us again — and if they didn't get busy there wouldn't be any coffee to sell this time. So you see, señorito, things didn't turn out too badly after all. We lost the new plantation and it will take us twelve years from the day we clear those animals off it before it produces again. Otherwise, I think you'll agree when you see the place, that things might have been worse.'

Indeed they might. With the loss of the new plantation we were back to where my grandfather had left off. It was no worse than that. My grandfather had taken over this land after the payment of the usual bribe to the President of that day. With a company of soldiers at his back, paid out of his own pocket, he had driven the Indians out of their caves in the hillsides, ploughed their miserable patches of exhausted land, cleared a few square miles of the wiry, tenacious, secondary jungle that always grew up where the Indians had once grown their maize until they had worn out the soil, and then he had planted his coffee and the shade trees. My grandfather was the ruthless Christian of his day with a fine singing voice and a taste for whisky and biblical exhortation. In his spare time he tried to bring the Indians to the light by forcing them to attend gospel meetings; but he got nowhere with them. My father was in some ways a lesser man, an artist manqué, who liked to regard himself as incurably impractical. He added the new plantation to the finca, but the effort exhausted him.

In remote places like this a few mastodons like my grandfather still lingered on, whereas the sudden change of climate had killed off their species elsewhere. Each of us in his own way, I suspected, typified our generation, although of my grandfather it was perhaps truer to say that he typified the generation before his own. My father already reflected the beginnings of doubt that crippled action, and he was embarrassed by what seemed to him the crude completeness of my grandfather's assumptions. In my case the enfeebling scepticism had gone further. The years in Europe had poisoned me with uncertainty and I came back changed, so that what I remembered of my grandfather's feudalistic posturings now struck me as grotesque. Perhaps it was the effeteness of the times masquerading as a virtue — the taste for democracy. There you go, I would think, obliged to excuse yourself for following your own inclinations. When the old man wanted to do something he went ahead and did it, whatever it was. He was sure of himself and he knew what he wanted. There would have been no heart-burnings with him. That was the difference.

Ignacio's great moment came when we set out together to inspect the finca. We rode up to the end of the valley and nothing had changed, but something I remember feeling when I rode here before I no longer felt. The coffee trees bore their small, unimportant flowers at this season. They looked well cared-for, and the soil at their roots had been freshly hoed. The plantations, which were not exciting to anyone who had not been involved in their creation or their defence, went up the mountain-sides to meet the rock and stopped in clean-drawn lines, like state-boundaries on a map. Beyond the coffee frontiers stretched a straggling mountain wilderness; a place of cactus and orchid and the sad, senseless cries of brilliant birds.

The new plantation was at the end of the valley, where my father had had to dynamite and remove several thousand boulders to uncover the earth. The Indians had put up their shacks in the middle of a half-grown crop of beans which were of the poorest quality. Here and there a few patches of maize were sprouting, and some of it was already yellow and withered. You could see at a glance that they had ruined the soil in five years. The Indian system of shifting cultivation without the use of fertilizers needed more space. They would have needed the whole valley, planting only a fraction of it at a time and then moving on each year to allow the soil time to recover. Nothing exhausts good earth so fast as maize. The whole valley might have lasted the sub-tribe for a generation, but after that they would have had to move on. It was their dependence on maize that kept the Indians of old always on the move and covered Central America with the ruins of their deserted cities.

We rode round the shacks, Ignacio very self-important, snapping questions, and the Indians cringing and their women peering out of their doors with frightened faces. They must have sensed what was in the wind. 'When I read in the paper that they were going to give us back the land I cried like a child, señorito. I wanted to go down and clear away all this mess, so that we could have put the land under the plough before you got back.'

A party of ragged-looking elders presented themselves, all self-abasement and wearing their ceremonial hats. They looked consumptive and the spokesman was taken by a fit of coughing as soon as he opened his mouth. 'What's the trouble?' I asked. I couldn't follow his quick, mendicant mumble when he recovered. 'It's the cemetery,' Ignacio said, looking frustrated. 'They're afraid we'll shift the cemetery. They put it right in the middle of the plantation. I don't know what we're going to do about it.'

The cemetery had been part of Ignacio's master-plan to save the trees, but he had not foreseen that the Indians would lay it out where they had. There were several rows of crosses with Latin inscriptions on them, and a corrugated-iron chapel with a resident priest whose single function it was to perform the office of the dead. The chapel had cost the Indians a whole year's coffee crop.

The priest, a plump and darkly seraphic ladino, came gliding smoothly to meet us, moving under his cassock as if on invisible wheels. He held out his hand to be kissed by Ignacio and dropped a sort of curtsey in my direction. I could see that I had gathered some of the aroma of property. This priest, Ignacio later told me, had co-operated magnificently with his masses and his candles in fostering the cult of the dead. Behind him came the caporal Sanchez, tamed now, a silent, hollow-eyed and servile figure, hardly recognizable as the man I remembered.

Ignacio chatted happily on planters' topics; about trees and prospects and prices, of clearing and replanting, of patient years and decades, of work and fulfilment and I let him talk on and thought of other things.

I caught my mind twisting and turning in the familiar search for self-delusion. I was incapable, I told myself, of burning down these miserable shacks and driving the Indians off the land they had taken over and ruined. What was the alternative if the finca was to be turned into a going concern again? The alternative was a further use of the recruiting system: a mixture of fraud and graft and concealed slavery. Or I could set out to 'attract' labour by high wages and good living conditions — the objection being that Indians were almost impervious to attractions of these kinds, and even if the labour could be found, the increased costs of production would make the coffee unsaleable in the market in competition with coffee produced virtually by slave labour.

This was the ethical front I offered myself, but behind it I knew that there were deeper and stronger objections I did not wish to recognize. I was seizing far too eagerly on each new difficulty that suggested itself to me. The fact was it was very hard to be honest with myself after years of pretence; but there it was — now that the finca was within my grasp I was shocked to find that I no longer wanted it. My lost finca had become the central myth in my life, the excuse for many failures, a peg on which to hang all kinds of vain hopes and promises, a solid piece of bad fortune to whine over in my cups. And now the comfortable pretence was at an end. It was hopeless to try to prolong it. I was not the man to run a finca. I hadn't the ruthlessness, or the staying power, or the necessary amount of guts. The idea of being imprisoned ten years in this valley watching trees grow began to terrify me. It made me shiver. I couldn't even have stood a year of it. This kind of enterprise required an excess of two qualities which I now totally lacked: youth and hope. Sitting there in the saddle in this vast, empty amphitheatre of silence, I could feel the melancholy of the place waiting like a tiger to leap out on me.

We went back to the house, and the servants had hung out the old, faded flags that meant that a fiesta was inevitable. The colours of the vanished states of the last century, of Austria-Hungary and Serbia, of Czarist Russia and of Savoy, were strung up limp with their washed-out stars and eagles across the unsuitable façade. Two long trestle tables had been set up on the flat ground behind the house where the tennis-court had been: one for the people of the household, of whom there were never less than twenty or thirty, and one — which perhaps symbolically was on a lower level — for the Indians of the finca.

They had barbecued a dozen turkeys and we ate enormously, washing down the turkey-flesh with home-distilled aguardiente which, as ever, tasted slightly of black treacle. The finca owners and their overseers, who lorded it in their absence, were much given to lavish, public feasting of this kind. I sat at the head of the high table with Don Anastasio, the ladino priest, on my right and Don Ignacio on my left. After that the male hierarchy of the household followed, carefully graded, all the way down to the bottom of the table where the usual finca small fry and hangers-on crowded together. The womenfolk served us, but did not sit down. The Indians would be invited, according to custom, to approach their table when their overlords had fed.

The aguardiente soon produced an emotional effect. The dependants at the bottom of the table got to their feet one by one and made the short speeches of gratitude expected of them for their food. Small boys in stiff new cotton straight from Armando's store were fetched to bow to me, and pledge their lifelong loyalty. Don Ignacio produced a guitar and sang touchingly about fickle love. The ladino priest, referring to the Indians who were beginning to gather in the background, started to quote the parable of the Prodigal Son, and went to sleep, bolt upright and showing his teeth. A full moon rolled clean up the edge of the mountains across the valley, there were fireflies round our feet under the table, and the first of the traditional rockets were hissing and popping overhead. High festivals were always celebrated more or less in this way on the finca. It gave the finca owners the opportunity of feeling like feudal lords. I remembered that this kind of thing had gone to my head, too, five years before. But now, in spite of the boost supplied by the aguardiente, I felt more embarrassment than feudal pride.

The thing that made this jollification different from all

previous ones I had experienced was that it had a double purpose. It had been put on not only in honour of my return, but to mark the beginning of a new epoch. Ignacio had arranged matters so that our peones were to be included in the fiesta if they felt inclined to come, and if they did I could see that it would be regarded as a formal act of submission. A group of about fifty, two-thirds of them women, had gathered near the second table, and presently Don Ignacio put down his guitar and shouted an order, and the servants came out of the house with pots full of steaming posole and bottles of aguardiente and put them on the table. There was a slight movement among the peones. One or two of the women took a pace forward and then stopped. The servants came out again carrying perhaps a dozen bowls. They ladled posole out into the bowls. The Indians still didn't move. Don Ignacio waved to them. 'Well then, friends, here it is. There isn't a great deal this time. As you know, supplies are low. So if you want it — '

One of the Indian women broke away from the group and walked towards the table. I noticed that she had a baby on her back. She reached the table and snatched up a bowl of posole. A second woman moved forward. All the women were giving in now, but the haggard, austere-faced men still held firm. The people at our table had settled themselves comfortably to watch the progress of the small drama. One of the women led her man forward by the hand and someone clapped. At this point I began to feel a choking sense of shame.

The group gave way now, all resistance broken. The men and women jostled each other at the table and struggled for the posole. I did not notice when they started to drink the aguardiente, but the effect when they did was instantaneous. The women went reeling from the table. Some of them fell over as if they had been shot through the heart, and I noticed once again that a drunken Indian woman who is carrying a child on her back always falls on her face.

There were shouts of laughter and applause at some of the drunken antics. When I got up and left the table everyone else stood politely, and Ignacio followed me into the house to ask me what my wishes were for the next day. I told him that I would be taking the train to Guadaloupe and he started to weep. What was the use of trying to explain to him? He would never have understood. By his own standards and by those of most coffee owners he was the perfect servant. It was useless to distress him by criticism based on the standards of a world he had never known. I also lacked the strength of character necessary to tell him what I thought — of the indescribable disgust with which my homecoming had filled me.

We were interrupted by a child who came running to tell him that the Indians were fighting each other with their machetes.

———————

22

I DUMPED my case at the porter's desk at the Mayapan, and went straight into the bar, and Greta was sitting there. She was half-turned on her stool facing the door as I came in, as if I were a minute or two late for a rendezvous. I went up to her, took her hand, and squeezed it with a considered lack of anything that might be taken for emotion. 'Hullo, darling,' she said. She lifted her face to me, but I did not respond. At that moment I felt a pleasant sense of self-mastery. Apart from that, nothing whatever, except some surprise.

'So soon back?' I found it helpful that the bar was full of people.

'I wasn't long away, was I?'

I settled myself on a stool, signalled the barman to fill Greta's glass, and ordered a gin for myself. I changed my mind. 'Make it a double one,' I said. She was dressed as tastelessly as usual, and I enjoyed a cool inquiry I held with myself into the source of her attraction. There was no use reposing any confidence in this mood. It was one I had experienced too often before. I could admit now in cold blood that her mouth was perfect, and I caught myself considering how remarkable it was that these lips, so repeatedly bruised by the kisses of lovers, should have kept their tender fullness and subtlety intact.

'Drink up,' I said. 'What happened?'

'Nothing. It was all too silly. Do we have to talk about it?'

'Not if you don't want to.'

'Well, thank heavens I'm back, anyway. Are you pleased to see me?'

'I'm always pleased to see you.'

'I didn't know it would be so silly and so — humiliating. They actually asked me to go.'

'That's what I should have expected. After all — you're not one of them.'

'There's half a dozen families living in the finca house now. I asked my mother if I could have a room, but it's nothing to do with her any more. She has to do what the council of elders tells her. I could see I didn't fit in anywhere. I could only stay if I married and they made it quite clear that nobody wanted me.'

The bar was full of Norman Rockwell Americans — the sort you always see outside the United States — with kind, shapeless, happy faces. Greta had not lowered her voice and I saw a pair of amazed blue eyes turned in our direction. It dawned on me that Elliot's season had opened.

'And what's the next move?'

'I don't know. I'm in a dreadful mess. Darling, I feel so hopeless. I may as well tell you that you were my last hope. I've got nothing to lose now by telling you that, because I know we're finished. I should have realized that it wasn't any use coming here.' There was a pulse beating in her forehead and I knew by the way her top lip was suddenly drawn up into a little peak of muscle that she was about to burst into tears. She would sit there and cry and there would be a scene. I felt hunted. We were surrounded by men in big, pale grey hats, and their womenfolk. They had all just arrived from somewhere and there was a crossfire of humorous greeting. 'Let's go to my room,' I said.

We went to the room, and it looked as though the Mayapan's new manager, who had been trained in one of the Statler hotels, had summed up the situation according to his lights, because someone had got there before us with a large bouquet of wilting, expensive flowers — mostly sweet-peas, which are very difficult to grow in Guadaloupe. I rang for the room-boy and ordered more gin. The room-boy was new and although I had never seen him before he already knew my name. 'Yes, Captain Williams. Certainly, Captain Williams.' He was an English-speaking ladino in the usual fancy dress.

I sat down, not too close to her. 'Is there anything I can do to help?'

She had recovered a little dangerous composure now. 'It's all right, David. I realize perfectly well how silly it was of me to come back. There isn't really anything you can do. I don't know — I just felt I had to see you. I feel so terribly alone.'

Something about my detachment was beginning to look to me a little unworthy, and yet I had to keep myself from involvement in her predicament, suspecting as I did that Greta's predicaments actually helped to attach me to her.

'You've always your friends in Guatemala City.'

'I can't go back there.'

'You mean you don't feel like going back.'

'No, I can't go back. It's impossible. I mean just that.'

'Then what are you planning to do?' I was beginning to feel nervous, and I did not propose to inquire why it was she could not go back to Guatemala City.

'I don't know. Shall I tell you something? I can't imagine my life the day after tomorrow. I just can't imagine going on living. I've nowhere to go, no one to turn to, no money, no future and no hope. I hadn't any right to come here and pour out my troubles again, but when my mother wouldn't have me there was only you. The only thing I've ever wanted from life was to be loved, and now no one wants me. I'm absolutely at the end of everything.' I could tell that she was biting the inside of her lips to stop herself from crying. One eye was dry and the other moist, and as I watched a single tear gathered and dropped half way down her cheek. I found this odd happening unbearably pathetic.

'Do you know why I left Guatemala?'

'No, you didn't tell me.'

'Well, there isn't any reason why I shouldn't tell you now. I was with Varela.'

'What do you mean — *with* Varela?'

'I was living with him.'

'Do you mean Werner's Chief of Police?' I had felt a pang. There was no concealing the fact.

'Are you horrified?'

'I don't know. I suppose I am in a way.'

'You hate me, don't you, now?'

'No I don't. Why should I? . . . I thought he managed to bolt to Mexico.'

'He was in hiding all the time. When he came out to visit his mother they were waiting for him.'

Well, so much for Varela, I thought. I was glad he hadn't managed to get away after all.

'They shot him, and some of them wanted to shoot me too. And even when they decided not to shoot me, they were going to cut my hair off — if it hadn't been for an old German in the secret police stopping them. Why don't you say something? What are you thinking about? Do you think that anyone else in my shoes could have done any different?'

'Up to a point — no.'

'When my father died I was left alone. What was I to do? There was nothing in Germany to go back to — apart from not even speaking the language. Have you ever heard of a girl — any girl — being able to live alone in Guatemala?'

'Wouldn't getting married have been the solution? — I mean right at the beginning. I remember a time when all the most eligible young bachelors were after you.'

'But they wouldn't have married me. Do you know why? Because I'd lost my virtue. As soon as someone had managed to seduce me there was no question of ever marrying any man of what they call good family. They're still at the stage when they want blood on the sheets. You know that. Without blood on the sheets you're *interesante* but never *distinguida*. Guatemalans aren't seen with women in public places unless they're *distinguida*. Why didn't you marry me when you had the chance? You know I'd have married you.'

'Injured pride, I expect. Tell me something. Were you in love with Varela?'

'No, I wasn't. I suppose I was attracted to him in a way, and he was good to me.'

Why ask such questions? Greta would never surrender any more of the truth than was forced from her. I thought of Varela, the cool-headed and cold-hearted. He was short. 'Little Casanova' they used to call him, and he enjoyed his nickname. Varela claimed that his reputation for profligacy helped him to get mistresses, and he was probably right. He was supposed to have gone in for torturing his prisoners, but who could tell? They always raked up these accusations about ex-chiefs of police. As far as there was any good in a man, Greta would discover it. She would even imagine its existence if it wasn't there. Perhaps Varela actually possessed some hidden grains of goodness. I didn't know.

About this point I found myself badly in need of another drink. I rang for more gin, and when the room-boy came Greta took the bottle away from him. She poured herself nearly half a tumblerful, and drank it neat in two gulps. 'Now I'm really drunk.' She was being rather triumphant about it. 'I'm absolutely plastered.' The fact was the gin had hardly had time to reach her stomach. When she was silly like this I could feel protective stirrings.

'I can say what I feel like saying now.' She produced a musical little hiccup, and I moved the bottle out of her reach after giving myself a shortish one.

'You know what's at the back of all this, don't you?'

'All this what?' I asked.

'The way I've been talking to you. My sordid past and so forth.'

'Well, what is at the back of it?'

'The same as usual, of course. I can't bear you to be indifferent. It kills me when you're indifferent.'

'I'm afraid I'm not.' A corner of my brain — the part that had kept aloof — had been considering this situation in a rational way, and had been forced into a certain admission. The germ of this particular love — that went so badly by all the rules, that was so hopeless, so foredoomed — was indestructible. It was always there, apparently lifeless but only dormant, ready always at the slightest encouragement to enter my blood. Perhaps, even, I fought subconsciously to protect it, secretly craving these recurrent fevers. If I were to defend myself I could only do so by flight, after which, separated again from Greta, the antibody I had at long last developed would quickly destroy the worst of the pangs. The thing now was to organize the flight. And in the meanwhile . . . I put my arm round her shoulder and drew her close, feeling the beginnings of a faint internal tremor. I heard Greta say: 'Why couldn't it have been us from the beginning?'

Why couldn't it? This was the great routine question that opened the gate to all the others. Dreamy justifications were forming at the back of my brain. I thought of a man and woman I had known who had been resolute under Gestapo tortures, and had collapsed cravenly at the first turn of the screw of love. The gin, too, had done its work well. I was ready to take the whole of errant humanity to my heart. I also suddenly found I wanted Greta very much indeed.

'Darling, don't send me away. Let me stay with you — even if it's only for a day or two while I pull myself together.'

I put both my arms round her, and then I got up quickly and pulled the cord of the Venetian blind, throwing the room into a cool twilight.

23

THE next day things began to move rapidly. The morning
mail from Guatemala City brought me a communication
from Army H.Q. relieving me of my command and instruct-
ing me to return to the City to receive my discharge papers.
There was also a note from Kranz, hoping to see me before
he left to begin his new adventure in a week's time. Aneta,
he assured me, had much enjoyed our evening out. My
replacement arrived with the same train that brought this
news. He was an earnest-mannered young man of nineteen
with a slight lisp, who, in the first five minutes of our acquain-
tance, told me that he was descended from the crusader
Geoffrey de Bouillon. As there was a great tourist strain on
all communications at that moment, I went straight down to
the airways agent and had myself put on the waiting list for
the Friday plane, three days later. Thinking about it afterwards, I went back and told them to make it two seats.
There were a few loose ends to be tied up before I left, so I
set about attending to them.

The most important was the Court of Inquiry over the
Julapa affair. I found that it had been adjourned *sine die*
owing to the disappearance of most of the material witnesses,
in the shape of several captured vigilantes. These picked the
locks of the town-hall calabozo in which they were confined,
and were seen to leave town on horses provided by some

mysterious well-wisher. I obtained this information from an apathetic secretary at the intendencia. Miguel himself, the intendente, was indisposed — i.e. too drunk to receive me. From this I took it that the affair might be considered as good as buried, and with the matter disposed of and beyond my power to influence, I resigned myself. It left me with little more to do in the next three days than say goodbye to my few friends.

A truly fantastic change had come over Guadaloupe in the single week I had spent away from it. All the seedy, wild-western atmosphere had been abolished at a stroke. Four more hotels had opened up, and every third shop sold souvenirs. The three vintage taxis had been replaced with a fleet of cabs drawn by horses with bells on their harness. The bandstand in the Alameda had been painted up and was occupied by bandsmen in green uniforms and Hussars' hats, who played Sousa and sambas alternately. A great many tourists were to be seen, although probably fewer than there seemed to be. If you have lived for a long time in a Latin country, where people on the whole are small and soft-spoken, Anglo-Saxons seem very much in evidence with their sheer size and their voices, which are like the cries of heralds. The tourists moved in little bands, wearing badges in their lapels to show in which party they belonged. They were whisked from place to place in ranch wagons, and when the ranch wagons stopped they got out and raked everything within view with their cameras, and dealt in a jocular and democratic way with the touts that came crowding round. Beside the tourists the touts looked very small and fragile and starved.

In Guadaloupe itself the Indian village was the centre of attraction. When I had last seen it only the framework had been put up, but now it was finished. It had been built in the pueblo style, which is chaste and simple and in fact the only really 'picturesque' Indian architecture anywhere, although it is geographically limited to Arizona. The occupants themselves were Mixtecs from the valley of Oaxaca in southern Mexico; small, button-eyed craftsmen who squatted under the poncho-hung walls, weaving, or painting their pottery. I learned this fact by speaking to one of them. He told me that they had been on exhibition before in Mexico City, and that they were all extremely unhappy here because the altitude had given them streaming colds. He thought that they would go back to Oaxaca as soon as they could earn enough money to pay their fares. They were well trained in dealing with tourists, and I noticed that whenever a camera was levelled in the direction of a woman she would pick up her baby, wipe its running nose on her blouse, and fumble for a breast. The tourists snapshotted, bargained happily for pottery, and told each other of their experiences that day. They were discovering the primitive highlands of Guatemala, and thoroughly enjoyed what Elliot had set out to give them — the pioneering sensation. Some of them were pioneering in a leisurely way, and others were pioneering under the pressure of a tight schedule which in a single day included Tamanzun, the Mystic Volcano; a Banana Plantation in the Lush Tropics; the Haunted Lake; and a picnic lunch amid the Ruins of a Lost City of the Ancient Maya (typical native food, optional). Even the scandalous cantina 'Thou and I' had been cleaned up and pressed into service, and a notice on its blood-coloured façade invited visitors to be Serenaded there by Colourful Musicians playing on Age-Old Instruments (10 p.m. to midnight. No cover-charge).

The hand of Elliot could be seen everywhere, shaping and reshaping Guadaloupe's destinies like a child experimenting with forms created out of clay. I knew that it would not be long before I ran into him, because in the two hundred yards of street, the square, the Alameda Gardens and that strange suburb called the Indian Village, of which Guadaloupe largely consisted, it was impossible to avoid running into people. What I could not decide was how I was going to meet this situation when it arose. Was I going to stand up to Elliot and accuse him there and then of murder? If so, I knew perfectly well that a chance meeting was a very poor tactical basis for such a stand and I would do better to look him out, present my denunciation in a formal way, and tell him what steps, if any, I proposed to take. Characteristically I put off any decision, and it happened that when the inevitable encounter took place I was with Greta, which was the least satisfactory thing that could have happened from my point of view.

Greta slept off the accumulation of weeks of fatigue and awoke at about midday when I got back to the apartment. We breakfasted together on some squashy, insipid tropical fruit and then went out. Now that I was to be released from Guadaloupe I saw it in a much better light. Greta, too, was transformed, and I knew that the familiar magic, or poison — whichever way you looked at it — was doing its work. I saw her again with self-deceiving eyes, happy to be deceived, as once more young, fresh and perfect. We were gay together, resolutely oblivious of the past, and I suddenly wanted to be involved with Greta in a number of simple, trivial, experiences that would help to fix this moment, with its happiness, in time unending.

We rode in a jingling, creaking horse-cab to the Alameda Gardens, listened to the blaring music, bought lottery tickets, choosing the good, balanced numbers admired by real connoisseurs, had ourselves photographed together by a hooded photographer against a backcloth of skyscrapers and spaceships, went on to the Indian Village and watched the sad, industrious Mixtecs sneezing over their labour. Guadaloupe was illuminated this day, under its dark, transparent sky supported lightly at the four corners by the domes of churches, and the summer pigeons twinkled like showers of metal parings overhead.

It was also a little unreal, as if the presence of the tourists with their big bones, their confidence, their pink flesh and their earth-inheriting voices had turned the town into a series of stage-sets into which other human beings were introduced only so far as they were necessary to enhance the sentimental background — dozing theatrically at their market stalls, kneeling theatrically on the steps of the church, propped theatrically drunk against a wall in the shade of their big hats. Elliot had called all this forth from the void of his imagination to satisfy the craving for unreality of these real and solid people. At that moment I was in no mood to dispute the universal need for illusion. The tourists sought and found it at its lowest level. The rest of us got it from such things as religion, opera-going and, of course, love — and the religious man, the happy tourist and the lover were all united by a single blessing: their capacity for suspending belief. Which was precisely the reason for my current moment of happiness.

Elliot, tutelary spirit of illusion, appeared to us suddenly in the flesh, with a mutter and wail of drums and saxophones — his inevitable musical aura. The jeep jerked to a standstill at our side and released him like a jack-in-the-box from its interior.

'Williams! Why this is a splendid surprise.' I could have sworn he was genuinely delighted to see me. I found myself introducing Greta.

'Miss Herzen, I certainly am pleased to know you, ma'am. I heard about your resignation, David, and I want to say right now how sorry I am you don't feel able to stay on and help us here. You certainly did a fine job with very little support. And oh — say, I expect you can understand how bad I feel about that business at Julapa. That must have been a terrible thing, and believe me, whoever was at the back of that has got it coming to him. Are you staying with us long, Miss Herzen? I certainly hope so. Miss Herzen, if there's anything I can do at any time — By the way, Williams — I was nearly forgetting — I hope you and Miss Herzen are going to be able to honour us at a little party I've arranged up at my place tonight. Just a few very special friends to celebrate the opening of our season here. Come as you are, of course.'

I remember receiving this with the bleakest manner I could manage, and I do not even remember accepting the invitation, although Elliot would have taken acceptance for granted.

'He's a very *friendly* man, isn't he?' Greta said. 'I think he's very nice — and it's easy to see how much he likes you.'

'What makes you think that?'

'Well, it's one of those things you can tell. I mean, it comes out in anyone's manner, doesn't it? Why, don't *you* think he likes you, then?'

'Yes,' I said. 'In his way he probably does.'

'I think you can always tell when a person's sincere.' Greta squeezed my hand again. 'You don't realize it, but everyone likes you, darling.'

A feeling about not eating the enemy's salt would have kept me away from Elliot's party, but Greta wanted to go and we were feeling too happy to disagree about anything.

Elliot received us enthusiastically. 'I certainly am glad that you and this lovely lady were able to come.' He gave us what I used to think of as his 'A' treatment smile, which in some way recalled the genial sugar skulls sold locally for the feast of All Souls. Elliot's voice dropped to a reverent whisper. 'There are some fine and wonderful people here today.' The fine and wonderful people included the travel editress of a fashion magazine, who was the most carefully dressed woman I had ever seen, the heads of several travel organizations, and Helmuth and Lisa Stern. Elliot especially wanted us to meet the editress, who was also the organizer of a travel association called Pilgrim Daughters. She was one of her country's most brilliant and beloved young women, he told us, and although only in her early thirties she had already shot to the top of her profession. He detached Miss Rankin from a group of her admirers and she turned on us the search-light of her interest.

'Mr Williams — they tell me you actually own a hacienda. How perfectly fabulous! I do hope you're going to ask me to pay you a visit.'

A four-feet-high Mayan prince appeared with a tray while I was explaining that we in Guatemala called haciendas fincas, and Miss Rankin, pleased and astonished, took a tamal and munched. 'My, these really have the most subtle flavour. What did you say they called them?'

'Tamales,' I told her. 'The drink is aguardiente.' My guess was that the leader of the Pilgrim Daughters had already eaten many tamales in the course of her travels, but that she wanted to give us the pleasure of believing that we were introducing her to a new experience.

'So this is aguardiente. Isn't it made from some kind of cactus?'

'No — sugar cane.'

'That's really a shame. I think liquor made from cactus always sounds so excitingly depraved. Miss Herzen — won't you have another tamal too? I shan't feel so greedy. They're quite irresistible — but I suppose you have them every day. I hear you were born in this wonderful country. Lucky you.'

Greta nodded and smiled her acknowledgment and, studying this confrontation of two extremes, I had a moment of revelation. Miss Rankin was like something made by high-precision machinery working to fine limits — the final product of her civilization. She had beauty, charm, energy and — freed from the deadly limitations of the cocktail party — almost certainly wit. Her clothes were right, her face and hands were splendidly cared for. She probably had exactly the proper amount of faith, hope and charity, and, as the Americans say, she belonged — and always would belong. She was at one end of the scale of success and failure, and Greta was at the other end. But there was a whiff of the sepulchre about Miss Rankin's perfection and an irrepressible humanity linked with Greta's unfulfilment. I was reminded suddenly of the biblical insistence on the blessedness of failure as epitomized by the beggar Lazarus and the Magdelene. Blessed are the poor in spirit, and also the muddle-headed and the purposeless and those not clever enough to take care of themselves. Greta had been lost in the no-man's-land between two worlds. Miss Rankin belonged to the well-organized future in which most human problems would have been safely solved.

There was a bluster of music between us, and suddenly Miss Rankin had gone. In her place appeared a man with the face of a whisky connoisseur in a *New Yorker* advertisement, who said with great seriousness: 'What all of us are looking for is ideas that put more carbonation into living.' He too then left us, and we put down our glasses and fought our way across the room to reach the Sterns. Helmuth was very angry. He pushed a printed leaflet into my hand. 'Of course this is absolutely immoral.' Lisa made a gentle restraining noise. She was wearing a little girl's party frock, smelt strongly of lily of the valley, and her brave expression and screwed-up eyes indicated a headache. I looked at the paper and read: 'The Indian New Year in Colourful Guadaloupe.' 'What's wrong with it?' I asked.

'Go on, read it, and tell me what you think.'

The man with the whisky advertisement face was back. 'Say what you like, we have a very wonderful new leisure market here, only waiting for the green light. You people ever thought about a uranium treasure hunt?' He put a tamal into his mouth, chewed, shaking his head thoughtfully, and vanished again.

'I do wish you'd read it,' Helmuth said. 'It's a revelation of how his mind works. Tamales? No thanks, I hate the sight of them, and I can't stick aguardiente either. What do they take us for — a gang of peones?'

I started to mumble through the leaflet. ' "The ancient Maya (pronounce it Mah-ya) have been described as 'the most brilliant aboriginal people on the planet', and the simple, industrious and friendly Indians who are their descendants retain in their folk-ways much of the gorgeous pageantry of their ancestral past. Guadaloupe's spectacular New Year's celebrations (the ancient calendar is still in use among the natives) offer visitors a unique opportunity to witness *and take part in* age-old ceremonies rarely seen outside Guatemala's remotest mountain villages." It's all the usual stuff, isn't it?' I asked.

'Go on and read the next bit. It's incredible.'

' "Staged in the romantic setting of the Alameda Gardens you will see the mysterious Deer Dance, the exciting Snake Dance and the Dance of the Conquistadors — dramatizing so vividly the victory of the Spaniards over the Indians. (Bring your camera with *lots* of film.) You will want to join in the gracious floral ceremony — " '

'My God,' Helmuth wailed, 'they're turning it into a battle of flowers.'

' " — which, with the ritual salutation to the sun, marks the culmination of these joyous rites." Wait a minute,' I said, 'I rather like this.' I read on aloud. ' "In the afternoon you may join an exciting excursion to the summit of the volcano Tamanzun to see the Mayan priest at worship before the stone idol of Tzultaca (Lord of the Universe)." '

'The Mayan priest, by the way, turns out to be one of the

Mixtec potters,' Helmuth broke in. 'Orwell was wrong. *This* is 1984.'

' " — or wander through El Mercado (the market), potpourri of multi-colored local life in search of treasures of native art. And then, perhaps, when evening sparkles forth and the fireflies vie with the stars, you will decide to relax in the spacious comfort of your hotel lounge while marimba-players make music for your dreaming." '

I have seen few faces as capable as Helmuth's of expressing disgust. 'Well, what do you think of that?'

'What do *you* think of it, Stern?' Elliot had come up from behind. There was nothing in his voice that fell short of his smile. I looked from Elliot to Stern, and Stern's face had changed.

'Are there any alterations you could suggest by any chance? I'd regard it as helpful if you had any criticism to make of my little effort.'

'No,' said Stern in a dull voice, 'I don't think I could suggest any alteration.'

'Fine, then. I'm glad you approve, because I don't set myself up as being a professional copy-writer. All I've tried to do there is to give the imagination a work-out. Oh yes, David, you'll be glad to hear that Stern's staying on here after all. Didn't you know he was going? Sure. He and Mrs Stern were all set to go off to Canada, so we had to look round in a hurry and find him some more excavating to do. Now he's a happy man again. Isn't he, Lisa?'

'Helmuth is always very happy when there is something to keep his brain occupied,' Lisa said.

'Well, I guess that applies to most of us. And by the way, David, I have an idea that the one thing that'll really appeal to you tomorrow isn't mentioned in that programme. I was going to make a surprise of it, but I have to let someone into the secret. I suppose that's the way I am. I'm bringing our people from the Project into Guadaloupe for the celebrations.' I could tell from Elliot's tone that this was intended to be a sensational piece of news, but I could not bring myself to show any interest.

'I figure the time's come when we can loosen the rein.' Elliot had managed to separate me from the others and I could see that he wanted to talk to me about his Chilams. There was something urgent and nervous in his manner. 'The way I see it, we're starting with practically fresh human material. We're dealing with a bunch of backward children. All right. We show them how other children play, and it's reasonable to hope they'll want to join in. Dancing's the kind of thing these Indians go for. The football games can come later.'

I was half listening, looking over Elliot's shoulder, trying to catch Greta's eye.

'You have to develop an appetite for leisure, otherwise work becomes oppressive, and everything suffers.' There was a note of appeal in Elliot's voice that recalled my attention. It came to me that he was up against some problem that was proving too much for him, and for the first time I felt the slightest possible interest in him as a human being. At this moment of inner crisis you could practically see Elliot fighting to keep his science-of-personal-relations façade from falling apart. My God, I thought, he probably hates everything about it — all that grinning salesman's pose of sympathy and good-fellowship. It had just been a matter of terrific self-discipline.

It dawned on me what his trouble was. 'They're dying on you, aren't they?'

'Yes,' Elliot said, 'they're dying on me.' The celebrated Elliot smile had gone now. His face had a puckered and defeated look. The Chilams had found a way out, and it had hit him very hard.

Elliot said: 'I've read about this kind of thing, but I've never really believed it could happen. It's like an epidemic, except there's nothing wrong with them. I mean, nothing the doctors can find. We have a subsidiary company running a parallel experiment down in Brazil. Same trouble. Work-force dying like flies for no reason at all.'

'Looks as if they'd sooner die than be turned into cash-spending consumers,' I told him. The remark gave me great pleasure.

'We hold autopsies. Negative results all the time. It's nothing you can measure or put your finger on. I mean the average brain weight's the same as ours. Structurally they're the same. Blood groups and what have you. What's the difference then? Why don't they respond? I just don't get it.'

'Can't your psychologist help you?'

'He doesn't even know where to start.'

'That doesn't surprise me.'

'I want to put a proposition to you. I've been turning it over in my mind and I figure that you're one of the few people around here with an idea of what makes an Indian tick. What would you say to coming in with us?'

I shook my head.

'You see, I have to find a new angle of approach.' The note of appeal was back in Elliot's voice. 'The way I saw it, you'd have a fair amount of time on your hands from now on. I thought maybe we could work out a pretty attractive arrangement.'

'Sorry,' I said. 'Your suggestion doesn't interest me.' At this point Elliot seemed to notice at last that there was some-thing wrong. He gave me a long scrutiny. 'Anything on your mind, by any chance?' He wanted to know.

'Yes,' I told him.

'Do you want to talk about it now?'

'Not here.'

'That's a pity. I expect it's something that could be cleared up easily enough.'

'It's a little matter of a certain machine-gun.'

'Oh,' Elliot said. His expression had slipped a little. Then he recovered himself. 'I think I know what's eating you — but you're mistaken.'

'You'll have to prove it.'

'I think I can promise to do that. That is to say — if necessary.' There was a pause and he smiled for the first time — rather defiantly, I thought. 'Of course, I hope it won't be considered necessary.'

24

THE sad people were brought into Guadaloupe early next morning.

It was like a planned military operation. A string of lorries rattled into the road running round the Alameda Gardens where Greta and I had gone to watch the dancing, and began to discharge the Chilams they had brought up from Elliot's Project. Then the lorries rolled away leaving little wooden groups of Indians all along the kerbside where they had been deposited. There were groups of short men and groups of squat women and children; all in sagging cottons. After a while some caporales came on the scene and began to shift the separate groups about and break them up. They were like herdsmen working docile cattle. The caporales were all ladinos. They wore big expensive hats and metal badges like sheriffs' stars, and their white blood showed in their height and in the worried movements of their hands. The Chilams were quite impassive. A caporal would take a man fairly gently by the forearm and march him to some new position, and then, released again, the Chilam would stand there looking at his feet, arms hanging at his side. They reminded me of the zombies of Haitian legend, resurrected by necromancers to slave mindlessly in hidden plantations.

Greta, unleashing her enthusiasms in all directions, as she always did when she was happy, wanted to see the group of Mams brought specially from Momostenango performing their Dance of the Conquistadors. She knew as well as I did that it was bound to be a poor affair. When Indians dance they don't do it because they like to dance, or for the amusement of spectators, but because they are driven to it by some inner fury or compulsion beyond the range of a white man's understanding. Caught up in this sudden tide, they will drop whatever they are doing, put on their vapid, smirking masks and dance on for hours and even for days until they fall down from weakness or starvation and others kick them aside and take their places.

Organized dances, such as this was to be, never came to life. The dancers in their tawdry velvet, their spangles and their feathers, trudged on stolidly to the sad screeching of a fife. They waved tin swords at each other, and their pink-cheeked, blond-bearded masks leered vacantly. The tourists broke into the formations of the dancers to discharge their cameras at close range. In the background Elliot's Chilams looked on blankly. The Dance of the Conquistadors probably meant as much to them as the spectacle of a similar number of men laying bricks.

We watched the Conquistadors for a half-hour, and then moved on to the Snake Dance. Here more masked Indians were taking turns to shuffle a few steps with what looked like a bushmaster with its jaws sewn up. The snake hung looped in the grip of whoever was carrying it, and gave no sign of life. The much reduced version of the Deer Dance consisted of men and women in unrecognizable animal skins walking round a pole. These last two groups of dancers had been imported from Mexico, along with the Mixtec artisans and the high-priest of the newly built temple installed on the summit of Tamanzun. There was a fair amount of discordant squealing of pipes, and this noise was soon heavily overlaid by a voice thundering from an amplifying system half-concealed in the jacaranda blossom overhead, which began a jocose explanation of what was happening.

The tourists accepted what was offered them with serious enjoyment. A Dr Shaw, who told us he was taking six months off from his practice to produce a book on Indian tribal customs ' — an interpretation, not a record — ' explained some of his photographic aims. 'What I'm trying to do right now is to capture spontaneous movement. Would you mind attracting that man's attention, sir, so that he doesn't look straight into the lens?' An Indian wheeled past, the dusty-looking bushmaster roping down from his thumb and finger, and the doctor's shutter clicked. 'That's fine . . . As I was remarking, it's the by-play of gesture that really interests me.' He fumbled for his notebook and began to write. 'Dancer with snake; one two-hundredth second at F/8. I find it pays to write these things down at the time . . . Now there's an interesting study.'

In the last few minutes it looked as though the caporales had begun to worry about the Chilams' lack of interest in the entertainment and they had herded them closer to the dancers, so some of them were standing only a few yards away. The man who had taken the doctor's attention was staring concentratedly at his bare feet over which, at that moment, several ants happened to be crawling. His head was a little to one side, as if this posture enabled him to study the insect movement more comfortably. 'The question,' Dr Shaw said, 'is of the right angle to adopt.' He began to move round the Indian cautiously, camera held behind his back, and then suddenly he went right up to the man and tilted his head back and looked into his eyes. 'Well, what do you know!' He looked back at us over his shoulder and I had a suspicion that he was pleasurably excited. 'This man's sick. He's in need of medical attention.'

I held the doctor's camera. 'I would describe this as a classic example of catatonic schizophrenia. Note the robot-like docility and the indifference to stimuli.' A caporal came up through the crowd, deferential as a well-trained waiter.

'*El hombre enfermo*,' the doctor told him. '*Si, muy enfermo*,' the caporal agreed. He took the Chilam by the arm and began to lead him away. Dr Shaw looked after him, shaking his head. 'That man is positively catatonic. He needs hospitalization right away.'

'They all look like catatonics to me,' I told him.

'Well, you may have something there too. I can't ever remember seeing a bunch of Indians looking as though they were enjoying themselves, but it's the first time I've seen them taking an exclusive interest in their feet.'

A rocket whooshed up and cracked sharply overhead, leaving a drifting lariat of smoke; the Indians were shuffling through their pointless antics; the loudspeakers came to life with a sudden crackling blare that drove a few dark butterflies as big as small bats out of the trees and sent them fluttering about the gardens. 'And now,' bellowed a huge electrical voice, 'those of you who do not wish to miss any part of the colourful flower ceremony are advised to make your way to the plaza, that is to say the square, where this is due to commence.'

I was bored by now, but Greta was ignoring my signals. There were important matters of policy to be discussed between us and I did not want these discussions to be postponed several more hours through the presence of our American friend.

'Hullo there, Mr Williams. Dr Shaw — I've been trying to track you down all the morning.' The travel editress had appeared, poised weightlessly like a hunting cheetah. 'Oh, hullo, Miss Herzen, are *you* having a wonderful time too?'

Greta agreed that she was having a wonderful time, and Miss Rankin measured her out a smile. 'I'm afraid I'm so easily impressed. I find everything so terribly *exciting*. Dr Shaw, I'm quite determined to attach myself to you. I must get some pictures of the flower ceremony, and you know how hopeless I am with a camera.'

'Why, that would be a pleasure, Miss Rankin.'

'It says here that guests will be garlanded in the traditional manner by Indians in gorgeous ceremonial robes. Doesn't that sound rather like Hawaii?'

Dr Shaw looked doubtful. 'It should certainly make a good subject for colour. What were you folks planning to do?'

'I'm afraid we must drag ourselves away,' I said, at the same time giving Greta the slightest of shoves.

The doctor's eyes saddened. 'Well in that case — just a moment — now there is an interesting shot.' As he spoke there was a flicker of movement right round the edge of my vision and I realized that all the Chilams had looked up at once. I saw the intendente Miguel coming towards us. He was bent under the weight of a box he was carrying — and I knew it was the famous box. He was staggering so wildly that he looked like a circus clown pretending to be drunk. After a few running steps he would stop, and stand there bent and swaying; take a couple of quick paces sideways to recover his balance, and then come reeling forward. His face was twisted and wet with sweat.

I stood there watching Miguel's approach. It was a few minutes before all the implications of what was happening sank in, bringing the sharp realization that what we were attending here had ceased to be a tourist spectacle. Miguel was outside this stage-setting of trivial figures; the inane cavortings of the performers, the mindless presence of the Chilams. His drunkenness, too, was not his familiar indulgence, but the holy and heroic drunkeness demanded of him — the only Chilam at liberty entitled to carry the box — for the performance of his people's New Year ceremony. Was this the result of some sudden emotional revulsion? Or could his apparent venality and corruptibility have been the stratagem of the weak and the defenceless against the enormous corruptibility masked by the justice and the law of an alien race?

230

I heard Dr Shaw say: 'Hold on just a moment, I don't want to miss that fellow.' I would have liked to make him see that what he was witnessing was not a proper occasion for photography, and that it called for wariness and even a touch of humility on the part of the observer. But I was too late. Dr Shaw had gone running to meet Miguel, hat in one hand, camera in the other, and one end of his tie over his shoulder. The jocular voice in the loudspeakers had gone silent for the moment and the Chilams were making a strange, eerie sound, as if they were all drawing in their breath through clenched teeth.

I saw Dr Shaw run up to Miguel, go down in a kind of act of homage on one knee and level his camera. Miguel stopped, spun half round to keep his balance, the black box balanced precariously — certain, it seemed, to come crashing down — righted himself and went on. The Chilams had stiffened and straightened up. They were moving forward, closing in on Miguel, heads held like blind men. Something entered the atmosphere that made my throat go dry.

The doctor came back looking unhappy. 'I guess he didn't appreciate my photography. Of course you often find that with primitive people. He actually spat at me.'

'They all seem frightfully worked up, don't they?' Miss Rankin said. The Chilams were closing in steadily round the staggering figure with the box, moving not so much as individuals but as a gigantic hollow muscle contracting slowly, and some of the tourists were struggling through to see what was going on. You could see the tourists bobbing about like carnival figures carried in procession, their heads and shoulders sticking out of the sea of Indian hats. From where we stood Miguel was no longer in sight, but there seemed to be little ecstatic shivers of movement spreading through the crowd from the point where he must have been passing. The Chilams had begun to talk in loud matter-of-fact voices, without excitement, conversationally — as they would have with one another, except, of course, much louder. I knew they were praying to Zoltaca.

'I really must go and see what's happening,' Miss Rankin said. 'Are you coming, doctor?'

'Coming now, ma'am,' Dr Shaw told her. 'See you good people later, I hope.' They went off together, before I could reply.

'I wonder if it might be an idea to take a cab,' I said to Greta.

'Or we could walk and see the fun. That is if there's any fun to see. I think something exciting's going to happen.'

'That's just what's worrying me.'

'Why — wouldn't you like to see something exciting?'

'Not particularly.'

'All right. We'll take a cab.'

'No. We'll walk.'

We started to walk after the crowd moving along the length of the Alameda, and we were a hundred yards from the edge of it now. The Alameda Gardens of Guadaloupe form a broad and verdurous T-piece with the town's principal street, which, in its last section just before this junction, is called the Avenida Presidente Barrios. The Alameda is about a quarter of a mile in length, and at this point we were rather more than half way to the corner of the Avenida we should turn into on our way back to the hotel. As we walked on I took quick stock of the situation, because the feeling I had at that moment was the kind that comes at the moment a revolution starts and one is waiting in the last fearful hush, hearing perhaps only the bang of a window shutter pulled-to, the hasty tapping of a blind man on his way to shelter, and then the clatter and rush of pigeon's wings as the birds go up from the trees at the sight of the first man with a gun.

Our end of the Alameda was emptying quickly. The dancers, some still wearing their grinning masks, had taken off their tawdry regalia and their animal skins, and were hurrying away, bundled up like discouraged rag-pickers. The permanent human furniture of the Alameda; the boot-blacks, lottery-ticket sellers and the ice-cream vendors, too, were leaving their pitches — and even the cab drivers, who slept through most of the day as a matter of routine, woke up and began to move off. These people, it seemed to me, whose sensitivities had not been dulled by schooling, had retained a certain animal susceptibility to the delicate vibrations that might precede the earthquake. Overhead a kind uncle spoke witlessly through the loud-speakers to the emptying spaces of rich treats of experience that had been prepared for the days to come.

The Chilams, flowing steadily like a migration of ter-mites, were filling up the other end of the Alameda, their noise now blurred to a low droning, and just before we got to the corner three mounted policemen with rifles in their holsters came trotting up the Avenida and turned into the Gardens to follow the crowd.

Greta said: 'Do let's go on. I want to see what it's all about.'

'There are about a thousand catatonic schizophrenics up there,' I told her, 'and if anything does happen it isn't going to be funny in the slightest.'

'I can't see the use of three policemen, can you? Let's wait and see what they do, anyway.'

'They're bound to be half drunk, which doesn't help. I wouldn't like to be in their skins if anything happens.'

'Come on,' Greta said. 'Why not let's go a little nearer? You can't see anything from here. Do you know, I believe something *is* happening. I say, can you picture Miss Rankin mixed up in a riot?'

'We're quite near enough,' I told her. 'A bit too near for my liking.' As I said this, I heard the tone of the noise the Chilams were making change, and ripples of agitation spread through the close texture of the crowd. At that moment the police kicked their horses into a canter and went in, and several of the jerking carnival-figures of the tourists were suddenly pulled down out of sight. The surface of the crowd seethed with waving arms raised high.

'Let's go,' I said. I grabbed Greta's arm and started to run with her. She hung back, protesting, but I got her to the top of the Avenida, and at that moment the crowd exploded raggedly and the three police horses came out in a gallop, riderless, and with a great jingle of flying equipment and a clatter of hooves. One of them tripped on a trailing rein, came half down, recovered itself, and went dashing by.

The tourists reappeared after the police horses had passed. They were running, and some of them were in line holding hands, as if they were playing a children's game, and their gay clothing added to this illusion at a distance. The younger and fitter people seemed to be pulling and urging the older ones along. The first to reach us were two athletic-looking young men who were half-dragging and half-carrying a woman between them. The woman was holding on a pair of spectacles with one hand, and in the other she clutched a shoe. She was in her stockinged feet. She seemed to be laughing quietly and every few seconds she would stop laughing and say, 'Oh my God.' Glistening, clear-edged rivulets of sweat had soaked through the soft, matt surface of her cheeks.

The white-shirted crowd of Chilams at the end of the Alameda boiled up again. Dr Shaw arrived with the second wave of refugees. He grabbed me by the arm, almost angrily. 'Is Miss Rankin here? Hasn't anybody seen Miss Rankin?'

'If anyone can take care of herself, Emily can,' a man said. 'Where are you going?'

'I'm going back to look for Emily.'

'Don't you be a damned fool, Ernest. Look, here she is — she's coming now.'

Miss Rankin was alone, in the rear of another scurrying group, coming towards us with her unhurried mannequin's strut. She was hatless, but smiling. As she reached us she patted her hair into position and began to sway. Dr Shaw rushed forward and caught her. 'They killed a policeman,' she said dreamily. 'They killed a policeman.'

The man who wanted to put more carbonation into living was panting by my side. 'I'm looking for the organizing host. Where's the organizing host? I left two hundred dollars' worth of Rolleiflex camera down there, and I want to know what he's going to do about it.'

' — and the chap with the box spat in Grant's face, so naturally Grant hit him, and he dropped the box and it smashed — and I guess that's about as much as I saw,' a young man in a white jockey's cap was explaining.

A tours official holding a paper came bustling up. 'De-Luxe Pioneers. Are there any more De-Luxe Pioneers here?'

The man who had lost his camera caught at him. 'Listen, are you the organizing host? I'm looking for the organizing host.'

'One thing at a time,' the official told him severely. 'I'm taking De-Luxe Pioneers first. Please keep together all of you. Miss Broadbent and Miss Salzburg appear to be un-accounted for.'

'Miss Broadbent and Miss Salzburg were going to the plaza to see the flower ceremony,' the girl in the stockinged feet said. She held out her shoe for us all to see. 'I don't know what I'm doing hanging on to this.'

The tours official checked his list with a pencil. 'Well, I guess that accounts for all of you. I'll leave Mr Updike to deal with the Regular Pioneers.'

'But I saw a man killed,' a woman's voice wailed.

'He wasn't killed, Mary, he just fell off his horse and knocked himself out. It was just a knock on the head. It knocked him silly, that's all.'

'But I tell you they killed him. They killed him in front of my eyes.'

There were several faint feminine cries of distress and the official said: '*Ladies*, I must ask for your co-operation.' His hand was raised sternly, like a conductor admonishing an irresponsible player in his orchestra, and beyond his head in the distance I saw a large human movement. The Chilams had in the last few minutes quietened and condensed, and now I saw they were on the move, although not in our direction. They were flowing steadily across the bottom of the Alameda — over the central flower beds, across the wide, mosaic pathway, filling the roadway and streaming through more flower beds and shrubberies, then finally beginning to pour over the low tile-decorated wall that enclosed the gardens. This crowd movement was as slow and deliberate as the lazy advance of rollers seen from afar off up a wide beach. The gardens were steadily emptying. The Chilams were on the move, and I knew that like a termite army they would take the shortest route to their objective — whatever their objective was.

I knew also that they would be compelled to pass clean through the town because, like so many colonial towns built upon old Indian defensive sites, Guadaloupe was on a tongue of land flanked by ravines. The Alameda formed the broad tip of this tongue, and the town filled up a bottle-neck half a mile wide with something like a precipice at each side. And I hoped that no attempt would be made to stop the Chilams from passing through this bottle-neck.

The tourists were aware now of this new turn in events, and the official whom I heard addressed as Mr Hickson was appealing for calm and order. 'Now let's all of us keep to-gether and make for the hotels. I repeat, there is absolutely no cause for alarm so long as we keep our heads, and I know that's what we're all going to do.'

'I demand immediate transportation to New Orleans,'

shouted the man who had lost his camera. 'You can charter a plane or do what you like, but I refuse to stay another hour in this town. And let me tell you, I'm going to lay the full facts before the Association as soon as I get back.'

I believe that women are less perceptive than men of impending danger. As we waited while the tourists were being formed into a manageable flock, I felt we were dallying in the shadow of a volcano which was clearly about to erupt. Greta was excited. No more than that.

At last the tourists were marched off. There was nothing more to do but to follow them. On our right, beyond the shade trees of the avenue, there was a foreground of rubbish dumps with vultures limping about them, and the foundations of a few new buildings that were going up. Through the hollows of this broken land I occasionally caught a distant glimpse of a white creeping advance of human lava, as the Chilams, slowed by their women and children, moved towards the centre of Guadaloupe.

'It's exciting, isn't it?' Greta said, squeezing my arm.

'A bit too exciting.'

'What do you think they're going to do?'

'Who — the Indians? I wish I knew.'

'I mean, do you think they'll burn the town hall and loot all the shops?'

'I can't see their looting the shops, because there's nothing really they want.' Except machetes, of course, I thought. And perhaps aguardiente.

'Perhaps the police will stop them.'

'I hope they don't try.'

'Don't go so fast. I want to see what happens.'

'You can see what happens from the hotel roof. That's unless some lunatic starts shooting.'

When we came into the plaza it was empty and the church bell was clanging. Baskets of flowers ready for the flower ceremony had been overturned by the church steps and the pavement was deep in red and white blossom. Just as we had reached the middle of the plaza four soldiers came at the double round the side of the church, trampled through the flowers and went up the steps and into the building. I recognized them as members of my cavalry patrol — whom I hadn't seen since I got back from the City — and I shouted and waved, but I was too late, and they didn't recognize me. Parties of police and citizens were busy in the Calle Barrios blocking up the side streets. Their method was to back up a cart which took up the street's width, and then smash the wheels. These side streets were in reality little more than alley-ways.

Miraculously I got Greta into the hotel without further resistance from her, and the servants barred the main gate behind us. The De-Luxe and Regular Pioneers were all on their feet in the smoke-room, bunched uneasily like guests at a cocktail party where the drinks have run out. We went through and out into the garden, and even before I had had time to put my key in the lock of my king-size loggia I heard the telephone ringing inside. I unlocked the door, we went in and I picked up the receiver.

'Hullo, is that you, Williams?'

The voice, slurred and clucking, was unrecognizable, although I knew who it was.

'This is Elliot. I'm ringing you because I have an appeal to make.' The line went dead for a moment and I thought we were cut off.

'Hullo, hullo,' I said. 'Are you still there?'

There was a great deal of crackling and I heard Elliot's voice a thousand miles away; then suddenly it came back in the middle of a sentence, '. . . ringing from "Thou and I" — just round the corner from the plaza. There isn't much time.'

'Go on,' I told him. 'I'm listening.'

'The Indians from the Project are running amok.'

'I know that. What about it?'

'There's a machine-gun up on the church tower, and all the side streets have been blocked off so that the Indians have to come through the plaza. It'll be mass murder. There's exactly one thousand two hundred of them, and more than half of them women and children. You'll have to hurry. It's a matter of minutes.'

'What do you mean?' I said. 'I don't understand you.'

'I told you. That crazy kid of a lieutenant is hiding under a bed somewhere, and his men won't take orders from me.'

'And they probably won't take orders from me either,' I told him, 'but I'll go and do what I can.'

There was a strange gargling interlude and then the words came out in a rush.

'You'll have to move pretty fast to get there in time.'

'I'll be there in two minutes. And in the meanwhile you could try getting some of the side streets unblocked, just in case.'

He was still talking and I hung up on him and went and found my officer's shirt with the two brass shoulder-tabs and put it on, without bothering to change the seersucker slacks I was swearing. I put a bottle of gin on the table in front of Greta. 'I want you to stay in this room until I get back,' I told her. 'No, I'm not taking you along. That's definite. And when I get back in about ten minutes' time we'll go up on the roof and see the fun. If any.'

I went out, and to make quite sure I came back and took the key and locked the door on the outside. Then I went to the office and took the service duplicate key they had hanging up on the board there.

The bells had stopped clanging, and the feeling one had in the completely deserted street reminded me of Salerno when we first held the town and we sat quietly under cover waiting for the mortar bombs which the Germans lobbed into the streets from the hills behind at precise intervals of one hour.

I walked as fast as I could without actually breaking into a run up the Calle Barrios into the plaza, and then through the crushed blossoms littering the pavement up into the candle-flame-pricked darkness of the church.

All the way since leaving the hotel I was practising on myself a psychological device. I was trying to make myself believe that I really was still an officer — to regain the easy inner authority I had felt before the instruction relieving me of my command had reached me from Guatemala City. More than mere play-acting would be called for. That I knew. I should have to produce a temporary state of self-delusion to be able to issue orders countermanding those of a genuine officer who, however feeble he may be, resembles in his poor sort of a way an anointed king. Soldiers are like certain animals, both timid and savage, who instantly sense the absence of true confidence in those who seek to dominate them.

Coming out on to the top of the tower, I behaved with a considered nonchalance. I ignored the soldiers grouped round their gun in one angle of the parapet and I strolled thoughtfully across to the opposite corner, which also overlooked the plaza. I stood staring down at nothing, counting the seconds as slowly as possible up to one minute. After that I wheeled round on the four men, lips pursed, breathing slowly and deeply and attempting a supercilious stare. I picked out the corporal in charge — he had been a private when I last saw him — and, ignoring the existence of the others, I fixed him with my gaze. To my tremendous relief he stiffened, pulling himself to attention as I had been willing him to do. He raised his eyes with proper respect to a level fixed at an inch or two over the top of my head. His hand came up in a salute which I returned with a movement of the forearm. I was happy to observe that his face wore that slight expression of guilt arising from a ranker's acceptance of the fact that he is always in a state of error. To be on the safe side I played the scornful officer rather heavily. I was trying hard really to feel this sense of superiority. 'Which of your men is number one of the gun?'

'Sir?'

'Well, I presume you know? Come on, man, wake up' (I thanked God they hadn't recognized me and responded to my over-democratic salutation when I crossed the plaza with Greta.)

'Ah — Private Mendes, sir.'

'Tell him to unload, clear the gun and prepare to dismantle.' I had decided that explanations would be fatal. The more unreasonable and even contradictory an officer's orders may appear, the more they are likely to command wondering respect. I realized that failure would arise, not from the nature of my order, but from an obvious collapse of self-confidence. There was a fraction of a second's hesitation on the man's part and I immediately attacked.

'Surely you know the drill?'

'No, sir. I beg permission to state we haven't been given it.'

'Deplorable,' I said. 'In that case do the best you can.' I waved my hand resignedly. A successful officer gives the impression that he is for ever overlooking causes for sternness.

I moved towards the gun, treating it with the right professional boredom, but at the same time I was listening with great anxiety for the Chilams coming down into the plaza. The gun, an ex-U.S. Army Browning, which it now occurred to me was the one that had been captured from the vigilantes at Julapa, was mounted on a heavy tripod and adjusted by a series of polished wheels. I kicked at one of them absently and it spun with a smooth low-geared action.

The men had closed in irresolutely. They seemed to be very slow in going into action and I had a quick moment of panic-stricken disbelief in the efficacy of my stratagem.

241

'Begin with the tripod,' I said, improvising wildly. 'In part two of the instructions manual particular stress is laid on the necessity of supporting the gun's weight before withdrawing the locking pins. I suppose you all know where they are?' I used a schoolmaster's sing-song, talking-down-to-the-obtuse voice, which is also favoured in the army, and with tremendous relief I saw the soldiers bend down and start to fumble with the wing-nuts. As a final touch, I dabbed with a fastidious finger-tip at a slightly scored metal surface and complained of inefficient oiling. Then I sauntered away and turned my attention to the square below, well content with the subdued cautionary cries of the men at work on the gun.

In this moment of culminating drama I found my eye taken with unimportant details of the scene below. I noticed the paler colour of the stucco over the filled-in earthquake cracks in the walls of the municipal building, the tilt of the green-tiled cupola of the *Merced* church, which at that instant wore a brief halo of pigeons, the sudden jerk forward of the minute hand on the clock tower, the wonderfully civilized design of the stone benches round the plaza with their S-shaped backs and paired seats facing opposite directions, so that two friends practically faced when they sat down here to rest and chat. Exactly opposite, dividing the classic, arcaded façades of the town hall and the police barracks, was the Calle Almas, a canyon full of hard sunshine with shadow-pallisaded walls, leading down into the plaza from the bull-dozed land outside the town where the old Indian village had been. While I looked up this the Chilams appeared at its distance-narrowed end and began to fill up the street

I had observed that twelve-power field glasses were included in the kit of the machine-gun and I went for them, taking the opportunity to comment sarcastically on the difficulty the soldiers were having in fitting the gun's dismantled parts into the three carrying-cases provided. The Chilams' advance seen through the field glasses was awe-inspiring. The optical effect of the great magnification was to compress the planes, so that the Calle Almas' length of a hundred yards or so appeared about a tenth of that distance. As the tide of Indians began to flow down the street towards us, they presented through the glasses row hung upon row of expressionless brown faces, all seen at roughly the same distance, the faces jogging slightly as their owners shuffled forward over the uneven flagstones, all dangerously close but not coming perceptibly closer. There was at first no sound of this advance — the Chilams had stopped praying — but after a while I began to hear the quick, soft pounding of bare heels on the stones. When they were half way down the street, coming on like a tidal bore, a coloured shape suddenly closed off half the field of vision, and lowering the glasses I was astonished to see a seller of soft-drinks turn with his barrow into the Calle Almas and begin to go up the street. Then I remembered the kind habit in Guadaloupe of giving the concession for this worth-while business to the feeble-minded. The brightly painted container of Coca-Cola substitute went up the street, and then, when the front rank of the Chilams was only a few feet away, the man seemed to understand the situation and he tried to turn round. I saw him wrenching at the barrow and then the Chilams reached him. The barrow was carried along sideways, as if on the surface of a toppling breaker. Then it turned over and was swamped in a foaming onrush. A second later it had disappeared and the smooth, unbroken front of Indians moved towards us as before.

The Chilams flowed steadily into the square below and filled it to its corners. The parts of the crowd moved very smoothly. Currents of bodies flowed, swirled and then ceased to flow as the space filled up exactly. A vast, slurred sound arose from the shuffle of thousands of feet over smooth stones, and sometimes waves of hushed muttering reached me. When the plaza was full the level of bodies in the Calle Almas ceased to fall, leaving half of the street's length still clogged with patient, waiting men. In the plaza all the Chilams had turned away from me and were facing the town hall. What was so strange and sinister about this crowd was its mysterious self-control, its seemingly instinctive ability to organize itself without the presence of leaders. As soon as the little eddies of movement beneath me had stopped I saw that the Chilams had placed themselves in ranks which were curved slightly inwards as if fitted into a segment of an invisible arena. The women had been formed with the children into a rough circle in the centre of the plaza, round the statue of Liberty. They were all watching the entrances to the town hall, as if in readiness for the curtain to go up upon the opening of a drama they had been summoned to attend.

An irregularity discovered by my glasses in the crowd's otherwise uniform pattern turned out to be several men in the front rank shouldering planks and fragments of what I supposed to be the shattered black box. I picked out Miguel, too, a hunched figure a little apart from the rest, and just as I had identified him the crowd shifted forward as Miguel went up the steps of the town hall and into the building and the Chilams forming the front ranks began to file in behind him.

In a matter of seconds the town hall was full of Indians. I could see their white shirts gleaming at all the windows. Indians filled up the veranda over the portico. They came and looked down silently into the square, arms hanging at their sides, and then they went back into the building again and others took their places. I could imagine them at this moment massing at the door of the armoury. The guards had long since disappeared, doubtlessly taking the keys with them, and I could see in my mind's eye the Chilams fumbling for a while with the locks and then settling down tenaciously, ingeniously, irresistibly, to breach the wall.

Then the town hall began to empty again, a steady cascade

of men pouring out through its three doorways to refill the plaza. I was surprised to see that they were empty-handed, and while I was still theorizing over what appeared to be their failure, six small shrivelled figures appeared at the top of the steps and I understood why the town hall — with its lock-up — had been invaded. The six shamans, easily recognizable by their grand hats, passed down the steps and when they entered and were absorbed in the body of the crowd I saw the ripples of excitement spread outwards until they reached the walls enclosing the plaza. I did not see Miguel come out of the town hall.

A moment later the crowd was on the move again, emptying slowly out of the plaza into the Calle Barrios. Then, as the plaza emptied, the Chilams held back in the Calle Almas began to pour down the street to follow the others. Once again I was reminded of the coherent and purposeful movement of certain insects which are supposed by those who have studied them to be not so much separate individuals as members of a single organism. It was all as orderly as an orphanage outing and as solemn as an *auto-da-fé*. It took half an hour to clear the square completely and to reveal a single piece of jetsam — the flattened remains of the soft-drink-seller's barrow — left by the passing of the flood. I never found out what became of the man.

A foolish and tragic incident occurred in the Calle Barrios when — as I later heard — a marihuana-crazed ladino rushed out of the cantina 'My Bet' and emptied his revolver into the head of the column, which absorbed such bullets as struck and then passed over him. No further attempt was made to impede the Chilams' migration as they passed from the narrow streets of the town into the suburbs and then into open country, going towards the mountains.

I heard the final, insignificant revolver shots echo in the Calle Barrios, and then the silence settled down for good.

245

The sun was still overhead, but there was a feeling of weariness and evening about the day. I dismissed the men and they went away with their disappointment, faces glumly averted, and then I went down and crossed over the plaza in the staring sunshine. I had a feeling of the passage of hours and days since Greta and I had walked together in the Alameda. Events had suddenly outpaced the stolid advance of time. A kind of lackadaisical curiosity took me into the town hall. One or two of the officials were already to be seen, seedy and dejected figures with sleepless nights in their eyes. There was a faint, sweetish odour about the corridors that reminded me of cow-byres and of the sweat of herbivorous animals. The Chilams had carried quick and economical destruction into every room; doors that had been locked hung from their hinges, and the ornate furniture that had impeded their passage had been reduced to a driftwood of gilded spars.

Only Miguel's office appeared inviolate. A knot of subordinates cringed and whispered outside, and I pushed past them and opened the door and went in. Miguel sat behind his desk in more or less the position he had been when I had first seen him. He sat there, a brown and stunted Hercules in black serge, his cheeks and forehead glistening with perspiration, his eyes fixed on me like those of a wounded animal, as I came through the door. He made an effort to get to his feet, and as his legs gave way and he fell back in the chair, a bottle rolled off the desk and crashed on to the floor. He waved me away, and although he was no longer capable of speech, all the hatred he felt for me was contained in his look. I wanted to explain to him how it was that we had both been ill-used, but his mind was beyond my reach.

25

T<small>HERE</small> was a delay at the airfield because the regular
service to Guatemala City was held up while awaiting
clearance of the charter planes that were taking the rest of
the tourists back to Brownsville and New Orleans. Helmuth
and Lisa had come to see us off and we had removed ourselves to a corner of the waiting-room as far as we could
from the continual nervous movement of the two grades of
Pioneers among the mountains of their good-quality luggage.
The tourists had infected one another with a kind of brittle
gaiety. They were proud of the dangers they had come
through, and were like children on a school outing who had
been involved in a not very serious accident which had added
temporary depth and drama to their lives. From cross-
sections of conversation we learned that they were on the
whole sorry to be leaving behind the blood, violence and
colour of Central America, but these slight regrets were being
overlaid by the normal anxieties of air travel: the hazards of
weather, the possibility of luggage being left behind, and in this
case the fear of some of the De-Luxe Pioneers of being allowed
in error to board the less privileged Regular Pioneer plane.

There was no mistaking Helmuth and Lisa's sorrow at our
going. They were both people of warm and quick affection.
Helmuth had brought for Greta the traditional send-off
bouquet of sweet-peas, and in a rather off-hand manner he
gave me a magnificent parting gift: a small, grinning

Tarascan figure in clay. 'Better not try taking it into Mexico,' he warned me. 'It's one of those that found its way out without an export licence.'

While the tourists surged around us with their cries of strained geniality, Helmuth described his part in the incidents of the previous day.

'Well, as you can imagine I'd have faced death sooner than go out with Elliot's goon programme in full blast, so I thought that rather than risk even going up to the ruins and running into some stupid nonsense, I'd settle down to a day's work at home. Then I was fumbling about as usual, trying to settle down while the servants were clearing away the breakfast things, and I noticed that they were talking to each other in Chilam, which was something they hardly ever did in front of me. I listened and I heard them say something about the box being carried in the procession. I tried tackling them on the subject — in a roundabout way, of course, because I didn't want them to know I understood Chilam — but they put on their usual dumb act. A few minutes later I noticed that the house was quieter than usual. They always make as much noise as they possibly can when they're working, banging buckets about and rattling the crockery. Always manage to smash a plate or two after every meal. I went to see what they were up to, and sure enough they'd cleared out. That meant it must be true about the box, although don't ask me how they knew. Lisa had one of her theories, of course. The point is that in the ordinary way they wouldn't have dreamed of setting foot outside the door without asking permission.'

'They never came back,' Lisa said, smiling sadly. 'I don't think Simona even waited to take her apron off, because there was no sign of it. They left everything else behind — even the shoes we gave them for Christmas. Helmuth laughs at me, but I know it was the marimba. A marimba started playing down in the valley before they went.'

'Nonsense,' Helmuth said.

'It isn't nonsense at all, darling. I remember hearing the marimba and thinking I'd never heard the tune before. I was actually going to write the tune down for the collection we made in case we ever wrote a book about Indian folklore, and then something turned up that had to be done and I forgot all about it. But I'm sure it was the marimba.'

Helmuth said: 'We'll let that pass. Anyway, as soon as I found the servants had gone I went to get the car out and go down to town, and of course the battery would have to be flat. By the time I got down there walking, it was too late. The panic was on, and I didn't see a thing. What I did afterwards was to look out all the Americans who had been on the scene when the trouble started, including the chap who hit Miguel and made him drop the box.'

'Funny thing they didn't kill *him* too, while they were about it,' I said.

'They were too busy picking up the bits of the box. Apparently it might have been made of glass the way it smashed when it hit the ground. Must have been riddled with worm-holes. And now comes the interesting part. What do you think was inside it, after all?'

'I don't know. What? Not the codex you were hoping for?'

'No. Nothing at all.'

'That's just what I would have expected of the Chilams,' Greta said.

'Would you? Why?' Helmuth asked.

'I don't know. It's in keeping with their attitude towards everything, that's all.'

'What do you think will happen to them now?' I asked Helmuth.

'Heaven only knows.'

'Do you know what I think?' Greta said, in her slightly misty-eyed manner. 'I think they've gone back wherever

249

they came from. They've rejected us and all we stand for just as they rejected the Spaniards. They've gone back to their mountains and I think they'll stay there until someone — perhaps not in our time — comes along with something better than Mr Elliot had to offer. I believe they've seen through us. Don't you agree?' I could see she was in a rather elevated frame of mind and wanted to identify herself with the Indians and their renunciation of the white man's civilization of the West.

Helmuth began to say something about his inability to feel sentimental about stone-age proletarians, but at that moment the loudspeaker announced the impending departure of the two Skymasters and the tourists began to swarm towards the exit door, all anxious in the way of air travellers — within the limits of politeness — to be among the first to board the plane.

A moment later we heard the bluster of the engines of the first Skymaster, and the plane trundled past with gently flexing wings, taxi-ing into position for the take-off. As it turned and lumbered away a blast from the exhausts caught at a truss of carmine flowers and held them pressed against the window glass. Lisa watched the beginnings of this impending escape from Guatemala with wistful eyes.

'To return to friend Elliot,' I said, 'my theory was that he had just gone off and got drunk. I went all over the place looking for him when I came out of the town hall. They told me in "Thou and I" that he had been behaving in a very strange manner. His voice over the phone was unrecognizable.'

'Now you know why,' Helmuth said. 'I'm quite convinced that the only reason I managed to see him was that his servant took me for the doctor. It was a rather eerie experience. He was lying in bed in a darkened room, and the first thing I noticed was that he kept his face turned away. Then, as you say, there was his voice. He seemed rational enough so far as I could understand what he was talking about. I ran into the doctor as I was coming out.'

'Is he going to recover?'

'Oh there's not much doubt about that. It wasn't a particularly bad stroke; although I suppose it will put paid to him as a high-pressure executive. It turns out, by the way, that he's at least fifteen years older than I thought he was. He's nearly sixty-five.'

'And how does all this affect you?'

I noticed the evasion in Helmuth's manner even before he replied.

'As it happens I'm not so badly fixed. I mean the year's extension of my contract had already been agreed.'

Last time it had been six months. 'For further exploratory work on the site?' I said, rather tactlessly in the circumstances.

'That's right. I must say I gave it quite a bit of thought before coming to a decision. There were all sorts of factors to be taken into account.'

Lisa came to Helmuth's rescue. 'As you know, my husband was very much against carrying on, but in the end we decided that another year would put us in an independent position, and then we could afford to look round for something worth while without having to think about the financial side. I suppose it's rather like an author or someone like that doing creative work, having to take hack jobs to keep himself going.'

'Of course,' I said. 'It would have been silly to turn the chance down.' I was trying hard to think of something to change the subject.

The first Skymaster roared distantly and slipped forward with tail raised towards the rim of the field. For a moment it was half-dissolved in mirage, then, rising clean-cut and steady, it headed for the volcano.

'And the finca,' Lisa said brightly. 'Any decision yet?

'Absolutely none,' I told her. It was on the tip of my tongue to add that I had even considered offering it to Universal Coffee, but I suppressed this revelation. There was something shameful about a solution of this kind. 'I really can't think what to do about it. Now couldn't I interest you, for example, in an excellent small finca? A going concern — could be turned into a paying proposition under energetic management.'

'In Canada, if you have one, I would be interested.'

'In Canada so would we. What we really want to do now is to get away from all this for a few months, and then see how we feel. The overseer's managed to carry on by himself for five years, so I suppose he can carry on a little longer.'

'But you don't even know where you're going yet!'

'At the moment we haven't a notion, and we shan't have until we get to Guatemala and see a very mysterious character called Kranz.'

'But it's Latin-America, at all events?' Helmuth asked.

'I'm afraid so,' I said apologetically. 'No Indians this time, though.'

'That's always something.'

'We're going to be together,' Greta told them in a tone of voice that showed that she meant them to understand that this single fact defeated and overrode all other possible objections.

A few moments later the loudspeaker summoned us hoarsely, and, exchanging wan smiles and gestures of leave-taking with our friends and promising to write and to return, we went out to the waiting Dakota.

The plane carried us bumping to the end of the grass runway, then, lurching forward with flame-streaking exhausts, it hurled itself at the rim of the tiny airfield where — just as the earth fell away into jagged gorges — the wheels miraculously lifted. We let go our breath, but immediately

— when hardly clear of the up-thrusting rocks — the wing dipped, and as we turned its tip brushed across the towers and domes of Guadaloupe that had suddenly shifted back into the scene below. I felt Greta's hand-clasp tighten. We were skimming the rooftops and yet so far away that the town's pigeons in their flight were a myriad of white specks on a glass interposed between us and the view. The plane levelled out, rode the crest of an air-pocket and banked again, circling to make height before vaulting the mountains. First the horizon sunk down, rotating smoothly to show us an endless recession of cloud and sky and volcanoes. Then the earth swung up again, tilting till it covered our window, and once more we saw Guadaloupe, but seen now as through the wrong end of a telescope, jewelled and precise among the knuckles of rock.

The familiar landmarks were there, but unrecognizable almost from this height and viewpoint. We were flying over Tamanzun, which had become an old, flattened breast with a vague depression where the nipple should have been. Lake Tenyuchin was a narrow puddle of black oil. The ruins of Utitlan sparkled like rock crystals on a dull scar of bulldozed earth. Farther away, breaking into the mossy texture of jungle, Elliot's Project had the appearance of a tiny cluster of white cells built up where it was by some social insect. As we climbed with engines snoring the earth lost colour and form, so that where the sun struck on plateau, peak and hillside it was yellow. The shadows under height-flattened mountain and precipice were purplish-blue.

Greta, relaxed again, looked down intently. 'Do you think we shall be able to see your finca, darling?'

'It's down there somewhere,' I told her. 'We should fly practically over it.'

I strained my eyes, peering down through the scarves of cloud at the veined and crumpled earth. I followed the railway track and found where the thread of the river passed under it. That would be Istapa. 'There it is,' I said. The plane's wing dipped, cancelling fifty square miles of mountain and jungle, and lifted again. I pointed down, trying to make Greta see the small dark cluster of geometrical shapes. 'Follow the river,' I told her. 'The plantations are on each side.'

'I've got it now. Isn't it wonderful? I'm so glad we've seen it. Aren't you?'

'Yes,' I said, feeling the slightest possible pang at the thought that I'd most likely seen it for the last time. In a reverie lasting not more than a few seconds I had something like a vision of the complex hopelessness of the lives being lived at that very moment ten thousand feet below us among the coffee trees; of Ignacio and his Machiavellian plans for self-preservation and the preservation of my interests, and the Indians absorbed in their funerals. I felt Greta's grip suddenly tighten on my arm. 'Please don't give it up,' she said. 'I want you to keep it.'

I felt a chill of caution.

'Let's go back there together.'

'All right,' I said, listening to the lack of conviction in my voice. 'If you want to go.' Would I ever return to the finca? I didn't know. Not with Greta at all events, I thought.

In fact the time had surely come to reconsider the past and the future, and to take perhaps one groping step forward in the process of divesting myself of self-delusion. I could not go back to the finca except as a man of stable purpose bringing reforms and a new life to the Indians, and before this could be done I must tackle the perhaps impossible task of reforming myself.

I had always seen myself as a victim of circumstances, one who but for more than his share of bad luck — the Second World War, followed by Werner and his reforms — would have been by now a man of solid achievement, a kind of benevolent patriarch surrounded by a numerous family and

254

a band of happy retainers. Thank God, I wasn't alone in my capacity for self-deception! Elliot probably thought of himself as a great civilizer who could succeed where the conquistadors had failed. Kranz in his own view was a gallant soldier of fortune, a kind of teutonic Odysseus, whereas I suspected that at least part of the reason for his flight from country to country was the necessity of escaping from the hell of life with the young mistresses he found in each capital. Helmuth was the frustrated scientist trapped into the prostitution of his work for unworthy ends — but whether Helmuth knew it or not, *I* knew he would continue in the profitable service of U.C. as long as U.C. renewed his contract, however contemptible the ends to which they diverted his labours. We don't change, I thought. The avaricious man never develops generosity; lust is only cured by the failure of the glands — and few fools have been known to turn from their folly.

And Greta, too, I sadly supposed, would be remoulded only by the slow wearing of the years. I didn't believe in the possibility of sudden reformations. It might happen — but never in my experience. What, then, could I do about this love for her, which only fed and toughened itself on bitterness and separation? I could mark time and await the opportunity to contrive one more ineffectual escape, or I could marry her and settle down with her in some isolated spot and in this way condemn it to death by routine and security — the death of the happily-ever-after, which in reality is cessation of pain and desire.

Now we were on the move I felt an unwarranted optimism. I was wondering what Kranz had thought when he got my letter and, following it, the telegram to say we were on our way. I could imagine his face. The more I thought about the switch-round in my attitude since that night at El Gallito, the more incredible it seemed, and I wondered what Kranz would have to say about it all. Kranz's offer, which had seemed so ludicrous — so unworthy of consideration from the point of view of a finca owner — was now almost magically clothed in feasibility. What could be more sensible than to go off to Colombia, or the Argentine, or wherever it was, taking along a charming but unstable mistress, with the dubious prospect of picking up some sort of dubious employment when, as and if, the present government were overthrown? It occurred to me at this moment that I was back roughly where I had started five years before, after the coming of Werner — an unemployed person, adventure-bound, with a little capital which would soon slip through my fingers. And after that — what? Ah, yes, what? ... And yet I was optimistic. The kindly fog of illusion was closing in again.

I got a quiet, ironic pleasure out of these few moments of ucidity and detachment. I was chuckling to myself when I noticed that we were already losing height, and just then the hostess came and told us to fasten our safety belts. In the distance I caught a glimpse of the yellow honeycomb of Guatemala City, wedged among its ravines. This flight lasts only fifty minutes. I hoped that old Kranz would be there to meet the plane.